Beginner's
SICILIAN

T0268440

Beginner's

SICILIAN

Joseph F. Privitera, Ph.D.

HIPPOCRENE BOOKS
New York

ACKNOWLEDGMENTS

Many thanks to my editor, Mary Beth Maioli, for her support and editing, and to my wife, Bettina, for her advice and editing of the Sicilian text.

Copyright © 1998 Joseph F. Privitera, Ph.D.

All rights reserved.

For information, address:
HIPPOCRENE BOOKS, INC.
171 Madison Avenue
New York, NY 10016

ISBN   0-7818-0640-2

Cataloging-in-Publication data available from Library of Congress.

Printed in the United States of America.

TABLE OF CONTENTS

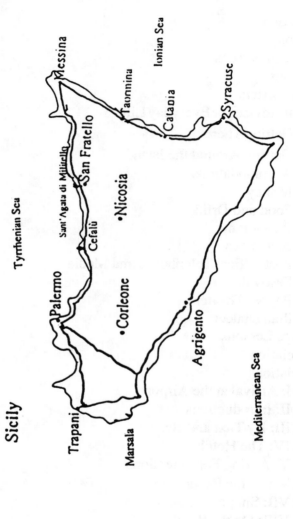

Sicily

INTRODUCTION

Sicily, long neglected by the Italian mainland, has recently been discovered by Italians, Europeans and Americans as a delightful vacationland.

It has a colorful landscape, it offers good, clean accomodations and delicious food at modest prices; it has a mild climate, the people are gentle and friendly — in short, it is an ideal vacation spot. Mainland Italians now flock to it for pleasure and relaxation. And because Americans, too, have now discovered it, we have thought of making available to them this very simple guide to the island and its language.

Sicilians learn Italian in school, for that is the official language, but, among themselves, they still speak Sicilian, which is their native tongue. Language holds the key to a people's culture. Use some of the Sicilian you will learn in this slim volume and you will find the pleasure of your Sicilian vacation enhanced many fold.

GEOGRAPHY

Separated from the Italian mainland by the Straits of Messina, Sicily is the largest and most populous island in the Mediterranean. It lies between the Tyrrhenean and Ionian Seas and, with its 9,924 sq miles, it is just about one fourth the size of Cuba. The nearly five million inhabitants (4,711,743) see themselves as Sicilians first and Italians second.

With Palermo as its capital, it is one of Italy's twenty regions, divided into nine provinces, all named after their principal cities: Palermo, Agrigento, Caltanisetta, Catania, Enna, Messina, Ragusa, Siracusa, and Trapani. It is an island covered almost entirely by mountains, a continuation of the Apennines; the active volcano, Mt. Etna, is the highest. The only wide valley is the fertile plain of Catania.

The island has a wide-ranging appeal. Palermo is one of Italy's most striking and energetic cities. Catania, its second city, is one of the most charming, while many of the other cities have well preserved remains of their past. There are spectacular Greek relics, especially in Agrigento, Selinunte, and Siracusa, which stand comparison with any of the ruins of Greece itself. There are also well-preserved mosaics at Piazza Armerina, which recall the lavish architecture of Sicily's Roman governors. On the west and north coasts one finds architectural remains of the medieval invaders, the Arabs and the Normans.

The Madonie mountains, in the north, are a beautiful wooded area which invites those who love walking. The simple, isolated interior is the island's most sparsely populated. The northern and eastern coasts have many delightful resorts; of note, Cefalù and Taormina.

2

Sicily's food is noticeably different from that of the mainland. It is spicier and with more emphasis on fish, fruit and vegetables. The flora, too, is quite different — it is southern, with its oranges, lemons, olives, almonds, palms and "Indian figs," as the Sicilians call their beloved cactus fruit. Day-to-day living is experienced mostly outdoors.

The Sicilian summer, when the Scirocco, the sultry, southeast wind blows in from North Africa, is not the most propitious time to visit the island. July and August are very hot, though relief can be found at the beaches, where accomodations are in short supply and the prices high. Spring is doubtless the best time to go, for then the almond blossoms flower in February, the fresh, succulent, strawberries abound in April and the island is covered with flowers. Every Sicilian you meet will proudly ask you *"Un è veru chi a Sicilia è bedda?"* Don't you think Sicily is beautiful?

Easter is the time for colorful festivals in Trapani, Érice and Piana degli Albanesi, and in almost every small town on the island. Winter is mild and a good time to be there, especially on the coast; but the interior, especially Enna, can get snowed in.There is good skiing south of Cefalù, at Piano Battaglia, or on Mount Etna itself.

Perhaps the greatest compliment to the ancient island in the Mediterranean is tendered by the mainland Italians themselves,who have discovered it as a beautiful and inexpensive vacation land and flock to it in greater numbers than do foreigners.

3

HISTORY AND POLITICS

Invade, sack and plunder...and tax, tax, tax. That is the key to
Sicily's history. Situated as it is between the European continent and
Northern Africa, and Spain on the west and the Italian mainland on
the east, the island has been easy prey to marauders and tyrants.

The oldest known inhabitants were the Elymi, Sicani and Siculi,
who gave the island its name. The earliest traders were the
Carthaginians from North Africa, who first settled at Panormus
(Modern Palermo), Solus (Solunto) and Motya (Mòzia) during the
eighth and seventh centuries B.C.

At about the same time, the Greeks established colonies in the east
of Sicily. Naxos was colonized in 734 B.C. and was followed by
Syracuse, Solinunte and Agrigento. These scattered colonies came to
be known as *Magna Graecia* "Greater Greece," whose wealth
eventually overtook that of Greece itself. It was a rich land they
exploited. Forests were cut into for wood to build vessels, the land
was cultivated,while the olive tree and the grape vine were
introduced from Greece. But there was rivalry and warfare between
the Carthaginians and the Greeks and among the Greeks themselves.
The Battle of Himera in 480 B.C. determined the ascendancy of
Syracuse in Sicily for the next 270 years. But then Syracuse itself
fell to the Romans in 211 B.C. and for the next seven hundred
years, Sicily was a province of Rome, which used it as its granary,
or, as Cato, put it, "the nurse at whose breast the Roman people is
fed." But the Romans also founded the large landed estates that have
been the major economic evil of Sicily every since.

After a barbarian invasion, Sicily was seized by the Byzantines in
the sixth century and, in the ninth, by the Arabs, who promoted
agriculture, commerce and the arts and sciences. They were replaced

by the Normans (1061-1072), who captured Palermo in 1072 and adopted it as the capital of Norman Sicily, adorning it with beautiful palaces and churches. The most striking thing about the Norman period in Sicily is its brief span, little more than a century. When compared with the surviving remains of the Byzantines, who reigned for three centuries or the Arabs, whose occupation lasted about two, the Norman contribution to art and architecture stands out. Roger I and his brother Robert, of the Hauteville family, conquered the island and were followed by Roger II, crowned the first king of Sicily (1130). His last descendent, Constance, married Emperor Henry VI; their son and heir, Emperor Frederick II (1197-1250) was a multi-talented ruler who acquired the name *Stupor Mundi* "Wonder of the World," reflecting his promotion of science, law and medicine and the peace that Sicily enjoyed for the half century of his rule.

After his death, Pope Clement IV crowned Charles of Anjou, a brother of King "Saint" Louis IX of France, King of Sicily (1266). The harsh, unpopular government of the French caused an uprising known as the Sicilian Vespers (1282), in which the French were slaughtered. The defeat of the French by the Spaniards was followed by five centuries of Spanish domination. The rule of the Spanish Bourbons was dull and marked only by the continuing abject poverty of the populace and the exploitation of the latifunda estates, held by a handful of wealthy nobles.

On May 11, 1860, Giuseppe Garibaldi landed at Marsala with one thousand men who, with the help of the peasantry, defeated 15,000 Bourbon troops at Calatafimi, and Sicily was free of Spain for the first time since 1282. Garibaldi turned Italy over to Vittorio Emanuele, the Piedmont King of Savoy.

But Sicily did not fare much better under Piedmontese rule. If anything, the lot of the Sicilian peasant was worse than it had been under the Bourbons. It continued in neglect and egregious poverty. It is little wonder that at the end of the 19th century, the overwhelming despair of the peasants was expressed in mass immigration to North and South America. By 1914, one and a half million Sicilians had left the island.

After World War II, Sicily was granted regional autonomy, with its own assembly and president.

There has been some growth in industry, and in 1950, though the discovery of oil near Ragusa and Gela and the development of refineries and petrochemical plants on the Augusta Gulf has not helped much. Agriculture, with the exception of the successful citrus cultivation in the north and east of the island, has not fared much better. Unemployment is still high at 15-20 percent. Perhaps the island's best hope lies in the development of tourism.

ECONOMICS

When the Ancient Greeks occupied the island, Sicily was considered the pearl of the Mediterranean for its lush forests, its sparkling streams and rivers and its rich arable land. But here, too, Sicily was the victim of invasion. The Greeks, Arabs, Normans and Spaniards unconscionably felled the trees to provide wood for the manufacture of ships. There was no thought given to replanting to replace what had been taken.

It would almost be comical, were it not tragic, to learn that the Arabs were perhaps the worst, though unwitting, offenders, for having introduced the goat to the island. As succulent and favored a meat as the Sicilians find it, the fact is that the goat devoured every shoot that might one day turn into a sturdy tree. From the ninth century on to modern times, the goat has succeeded in turning the lush land into one with large arid areas, and stark naked rocks and stones, where trees grew and streams and rivers flowed. Now, wooded sections are to be found only in the mountainous areas southeast of Messina.

From early times to the present day, Sicily's economy has been based on agriculture, hampered by the lack of rivers and streams for irrigation. Its production consists of the following: grains, mostly wheat, the envy of Europe; olives and olive oil, dark green, rich and heavy, thought by many to be the best produced in Italy; grapes and wines, many as good as the best of Piedmont and Tuscany, but as yet undiscovered and not properly promoted, though it has long been famous for its dessert wines, the Marsala, the Passito of Pantelleria and the Moscato of Syracuse; cotton, introduced by the Saracens in the ninth century; pasture land for the raising of sheep, cows, goats, swine and horses, its cheeses rank with Italy's best, but are unfamiliar to the rest of Italy because of the

7

limited production; citrus fruit, the best in the world, and almonds. Sicily provides 67% of the oranges produced in Italy, 51% of the tangerines and 92% of the lemons. The most intensely cultivated fruit tree is the almond, which provides 74% of the Italian production, figs, hazel-nuts and peaches. Vegetables and legumes are cultivated in the coastal areas, especially in the east. Cotton is the most important used by industry. Sicily enjoys a monopoly, providing, as it does, 100% of the Italian production.

Since it was introduced by the Saracens, the fishing of tuna has been an important Sicilian activity especially on the west coast. Sicilian tuna packed in olive oil is the best produced anywhere. The swordfish dominates the fishing off the Straits of Messina. The Sicilian fondness for these two regal fish is reflected in the many succulent dishes in the island's cuisine.

Together with Sardinia and Tuscany, Sicily is one of the few Italian regions which have mineral deposits of any importance. The major mining industry in Sicily has been for centuries that of sulphur. In the nineteenth century, the parents and in-laws of Nobel Prize Laureate Luigi Pirandello were among the major producers of sulphur. Its production was so abundant that it dominated the world market. But the production, because it used antiquated methods, continued to become more costly and could no longer compete with that produced by the States and Mexico, which used a more modern technology.

After World War II, large deposits of petroleum and methane gas were discovered in the area around Ragusa and Gela. The first well began to produce in 1957. From that point on the island has seen considerable expansion of the petroleum, petrochemical and thermoelectric industries with large establishments in Gela, Augusta and Siracusa.

Thanks to the recent discovery of potassium salts in the interior, large quantities are being used in the production of fertilizers in the Gela area.

ARTS AND LETTERS

There are two types of architecture in Sicily; the first is an amalgam of Arabic and Byzantine, modified by the Normans, found in churches and public buildings. Prominent among these is the Cathedral at Monreale, on the outskirts of Palermo, with its adjoining Benedictine monastery. The ceiling and walls of the cathedral are covered with a striking mosaic, depicting biblical scenes, dominated, at the top, by the figure of Christ, all in the Byzantine style. Mosaics have been popular in Sicily through the ages and one can find, in tourist areas like Taormina, small shops which sell artistic mosaic renditions, all beautifully framed.

The second type of architecture is much more in evidence, for it was developed at a later date; it is the Sicilian Baroque, which flourished during the eighteenth century when the island was ruled by the Spanish Bourbons, the House of Savoy, the Austrian Hapsburgs and the Bourbons of Naples. It is a style which has been described as reflection, warmth and ebullience, gaiety, energy, freedom and fantasy. All are used to describe ornate façades with wide balconies and sumptuous staircases, found in public buildings and the *palazzi* of the rich.

Sicily has given many fine painters to the world. Of these, one of the great painters of the Renaissance was Antonello da Messina, born in Messina, as his name indicates, around 1430. He began painting in Sicily in 1446 and left for Venice in 1475, where he lived for almost two years, during which time his influence was such that it changed Venetian painting. Antonello is thought to have introduced oil painting to Venice and Italy. One of the first artists to have painted in oil, he probably learned the technique either from Calantonio, a master with whom he studied in 1456 or some Spanish painter trained in the Netherlands.

Certainly, the most famous of Antonello's works is the *Virgin Annunciate,* which can be seen in Palermo's national museum. It was painted circa 1465 and represents one of the masterpieces of the 15th century. Also famed are his *Portrait of a Man* and *The Crucifixion,* both at the London's National Gallery.

Sicilians are a musical people; there is no family that does not boast one or two musicians. Many an evening is whiled away to the folk tunes played by two or more musicians on the violin, mandolin, guitar or clarinet. There are informal schools of music in most towns where one or several accomplished musicians teach one or more instruments. Frequently, it is one *prufissuri* (professor) who will teach five, six or a dozen instruments, in all of which he is competent.

Each town has at least one brass band, made up of clarinets, trumpets, horns, tubas, drums, etc. These groups give concerts, which feature excerpts from Italian opera, during the many religious festivals; and, in smaller number, they accompany a funeral dirge, playing a solemn, slow-paced music, composed anonymously over the centuries.

But the star of music in Sicily was Vincenzo Bellini, born in Catania in 1801 who, during his short life (dead in 1835), wrote eleven operas, all successfully staged. He is especially remembered for *I Capulettti ed i Montecchi, La Sonnambula, Norma* and *I Puritani,* all of which are still performed in opera houses throughout the world.

It was the great Federick II, born in 1194, who formed the Sicilian School of Poetry, the first school of poetry in all of Italy, which modelled itself on the poetry of the Troubadours of Provence, looked up to by Dante himself. The great Tuscan poet immortalized

11

Pier Della Vigna, one of the best, in his *Inferno*. Dante mentions Giacomo Da Lentini in the *Divine Comedy* and quotes him in his *De Vulgari Eloquentia*. Giacomo is thought to have invented the sonnet, which he introduced in the poem beginning with the line "Love is a longing born within the heart."

The writing of poetry in the dialect has continued through the centuries, much of it oral, some recorded. Among the latter is the work of Vincenzo Guarnacia (1899-1953), who is especially noted for his *Sicilian Octaves*, written, with great longing for his native land, during World War II. The opening verse of these 33 octaves indicates the poignancy of the lines that follow"

> Absence is a drop of bitter water
> That slowly drips into the heart...

Sicilians have been active in the theater. During the first decade of the twentieth century, several theatrical troupes performed plays written in Sicilian, both on the island and on the mainland. The most prominent of these producer-playrights was Nino Martoglio, a prolific dramatist who first nudged Luigi Pirandello into writing twelve plays in Sicilian. These formed the nucleus of his entire production of 56 plays, which helped him earn the Nobel Prize for Literature in 1934.

But Pirandello, if pre-eminent as a dramatist, was also a renowned novelist and writer of short stories, *The Late Mattia Pascal; One, No One, A Hundred Thousand*, to mention but two of his many works.

The most revered of the Sicilian novelists was Giovanni Verga (1840-1922) whose style is characterized by simplicity, strict attention to accuracy and sympathy with the poverty and struggles of

12

Sicilian peasant folk. His best known works are *Cavalleria rusticana*, *The House by the Medlar Tree* and *Maestro Don Gesualdo*. A dramatization of *Cavalleria rusticana* was produced in 1884 on which Mascagni based his opera, *Cavalleria rusticana*, in 1890.

Perhaps the best known of all the novelists is Giuseppe Tomasi di Lampedusa (1896-1957) for *The Leopard*, which appeared posthumously in 1958 to immediate critical acclaim. The novel describes life among the nobles at the turn of the century, when certain traditional values of Sicilian life had begun to change and disappear.

Of great stature in the contemporary scene are Leonardo Sciascia and Elio Vittorini. It should be noted that all Sicilian authors have written in Italian, with the exception of Nino Martoglio and Pirandello who wrote and produced plays in the dialect.

PRACTICAL ADVICE FOR EVERYDAY LIFE

GETTING THERE

1. By Air

Alitalia, Italy's national airline, has the most varied routes between the US and Italy. It flies daily from New York, Boston, Miami, Chicago and Los Angeles to Milan and Rome. The American airlines fly to Milan and Rome from fewer American cities: *Delta Airlines* flies daily from New York, Chicago and Los Angeles; *TWA* flies daily from Los Angeles and Chicago, via New York; *American Airlines* flies directly to Milan from Chicago and to Rome and Venice, via London, Brussels or Zurich. If you wish to make a European stop-over, you have the choice of the following airlines with service to Rome and Milan: *British Airways* (via London); *Air France* (via Paris); *Lufthansa* (via Frankfurt or Munich); *Iberia* (via Madrid); *Sabena* (via Brussels); *Swissair* (via Zurich); *Icelandair* (via Luxembourg); *KLM* (via Amsterdam): and *SAS* (via Copenhagen).

Direct flights from New York or Boston take about nine hours, twelve hours from Chicago and fifteen from Los Angeles. Add another hour and fifteen minutes to three hours for the connecting flight to Sicily.

Round-trip fares to Rome or Milan vary little between airlines. The cheapest round-trip fare starts at around $650, if travelling in mid-week in low season (November-March), rising to around $750 during the shoulder seasons (September-October and April-May) and up to $900 during the summer months. Add about $200 to these fares if flying from Los Angeles and $100 if flying out of Chicago. Add-on fares from Milan or Rome to Palermo or Catania range from

$100-200, depending on the season and the airline.

2. Through Packaged Tours

The following agencies offer group travel and tours in Sicily:

Adventure Center (1-800-227-8747) offers a "Sicilian Volcano" hiking tour, starting at $800, not including airfare.
American Express Vacations (1-800-241-1700), individual and escorted tours anywhere in Italy, including Sicily.
Archeological Tours 271 Madison Ave., NY, NY 10016 (212-986-3054). Escorted archeological tours of Sicily, from 14 to 17 days, around $4,000.
CIT Tours 342 Madison Ave., NY, NY 10173 (212-697-2100) Escorted Sicilian tours.
Italiatour (1-800-237-0517) in conjunction with *Alitalia*, offers fly-drive tours and escorted and individual tours.
Globus-Cosmos (1-800-221-0090), escorted and individual tours of Italy and Sicily; prices start at $1300.
Mountain Travel-Sobek (1-800-227-2384), offers a "Sicilian Adventure," a hike to the summit of Mt Etna and a visit to the Aeolian islands, for around $2250, excluding airfare.

GETTING AROUND ON THE ISLAND

Sicily is a small island and distances are short. One can travel across the island from, say, Siracusa to Tràpani, in one day. Trains are generally slow and cover only the main cities; buses reach the more remote areas,but,with few exceptions, do not run on Sundays. However, the prices for public transportation are among the cheapest in Europe.

15

1. By Train

The trains are operated by the *Ferrovie dello Stato (FS)*, the Italian State Railways. For the most part, trains do leave on time.

There are four types of trains:
<u>Intercity</u>, which link the main Sicilian centers with each other: reservations and a 30% supplement, payable in advance, are obligatory.
<u>Espresso</u>, call only at the larger stations.
<u>Diretto</u>, stop at most stations, and finally, the
<u>Regionale</u> (also called the Locale) stop at every station (to be avoided)
N B: Tickets must be validated (punched in a machine on the station) an hour before boarding. It pays to have a seat reservation (*prenotazione*) on the main routes. Note the following signs displayed on the boards at the station: *Partenze*, Departures; *Arrivi*, Arrivals; *In Ritardo*, Delayed.
The **price** of tickets is reasonable; tickets are charged by the kilometer. A 300 kilometer run (from Siracusa to Caltanisetta, for example) costs 21,000 Lire ($12.54)

2. By Bus

Buses are usually quicker and more reliable than trains. They will go almost anywhere you want to go. A trip which crosses the island, say, from Catania to Palermo, costs around 16,000 Lire (just under $10.00). There are two main companies, *SAIS* and *AST*, which, between them, cover most of the island. City buses are quite cheap, charging a flat fare of 800-1300 Lire (50-75 cents). Bus terminals are scattered all over town, though buses usually pull up in one particular plaza. Ask for the *Autostazione* if you want a bus.

3. By Car

Car rental in Sicily is expensive, around $380 a week, plus fuel, with unlimited mileage. It is best to arrange for a car rental with one of the following agencies, which can arrange pickup in Catania and Palermo.

Auto Europe 1-800-223-5555
Avis 1-800-331-1084
Budget 1-800-527-0700
Dollar 1-800-421-6868
Europe by Car 1-800-223-1516
Hertz 1-800-654-3001

ACCOMMODATIONS

By and large, accomodations are slightly cheaper in Sicily than on the mainland; they are officially graded and their tariffs are fixed by law. You can expect to pay around $30 a night for two, sometimes even less than that. Hotels are fairly abundant in the large centers, less so in the smaller ones, while there are many towns, with a population of under 10,000 which have none. You can expect to pay a bit more for a room with a bathroom or shower.

MONEY

The lira is Italy's common currency. The exchange will vary up or down at around 1,675 L to the dollar. Traveller's checks and credit cards are accepted at all hotels in the larger centers. Traveller's checks can be exchanged for liras at any bank.

FOOD AND DRINK

Food and drink are good and inexpensive in Sicily. One can get a good meal anywhere on the island, accompanied by a glass or bottle of good local wine.

Historically, Sicilian cuisine has been held in high regard and still is, leaning heavily on locally produced foodstuffs and what can be fished out of the sea. Pasta, with tomato sauce or a variety of locally produced sauces, wild fennel, tuna and olive-oil cured black olives, with meatballs or sausages, or even a sauce with whole medium-sized potatoes cooked in it. The variety is legion. Tuna, swordfish, capers, olives, raisins are to be found in many dishes. Oranges, persimmons, artichokes, asparagus are found the year round in most of the island. Among the fruit, the prickly pear, orginally imported from Mexico by the Spaniards, is one of the favorites. The Arab influence is evident in the profusion of sweets and desserts — marzipan, cassata and cannoli, made with sweet ricotta. The best time to sample the more unusual dishes and desserts is during the festivals in which food plays a large role.

Breakfast for most Sicilians consists of *café au lait,* fresh bread with butter and jam or a cappuccino and a pastry and can be eaten, standing, at a bar.

Pizzerias

Outside Naples, which invented the pizza, the best place to eat pizza is in Sicily, which uses the old-fashioned wood-fired oven which produces a bubbly dough. No deep-dish pizza, but flat and toasted just right, mostly tomato and cheese and not with the wide variety of toppings to which we are accustomed in the States. Cost, around L5,000, for the fancier, from 7,000 to 10,000 liras.

Restaurants

Full meals can be taken at *trattorias* or *ristoranti*. The first is cheaper and features homestyle cooking. Restaurants are more upscale, and have tablecloths and waiters.

As on the mainland, a meal (*pranzo*, lunch, *cena*, dinner) starts with an antipasto. A plateful of cold dishes will cost you around L10,000. A full meal starts with *il primo*, soup or pasta (around L6,000-12,000) and goes on to *il secondo*, the meat or fish dish (around L12,000-18,000).Side dishes (*i contorni*) are ordered separately. Ask for the bill (*il conto*) at the end of the meal. It will include a cover charge (*bread and cover*), around L1,500-3,000 per person; service (*servizio*), another 10 percent (though it can go as high as 15 or even 20 percent). You won't be expected to tip if service is included; otherwise, leave a 10 percent tip (not expected at pizzerias and trattorias.

Beverages

Sicilians are not hard drinkers. You will rarely see a drunk in public. Yet Sicilians drink wine from childhood, but only as part of the main evening meal, or, on Sundays and holidays, at midday, but always with food. Families that have access to a country place or who live in the country, make enough wine in the Fall to last them throughout the year. Most small towns have *cooperativi viniculi* wine cooperatives, which buy from the residents or from farmers, *mustu,* the juice of crushed grapes, which they ferment and develop into table wine or fine wines for sale locally or thoughtout the island. Some of Sicily's finest wines are produced in this manner. While Sicily has not yet developed a sophisticated wine industry, it produces and bottles wines, many of which, can compete in quality with the best wines from up north. One of these, *Marsala,* has long been known as one of Italy's finest dessert wines. It is interesting to note that it was developed and merchandised by the British in much the same way that they developed sherry in Spain and port in Portugal.For the traveller who is accustomed to a pre-prandial cocktail, restaurants will offer the most varied hard drinks available anywhere in the world.

For those who wish to quench their thirst with soft drinks, Sicily offers a host of delicious concoctions made from a wide selection of fresh fruit. Or one can order a *spremuta,* a fresh fruit — orange, lemon, or grapefruit, squeezed on order at the bar.

Walking down the street in the main square, one would think he were in Brazil, from the strong fragrance of coffee. Sicilians are coffee drinkers. Their coffee is usually the strong *espresso,* or the *cappucino* or *caffelatte, espresso* mixed with warm milk.

Then there is the *frullato,* a fresh fruit-shake made with several fruit. Or the *granita,* a crushed ice drink made with coffee or a variety of fruit juices. *Acqua minerale,* mineral water, is always offered in restaurants, as an alternative to wine or to mix with it.

POST OFFICE, TELEPHONES AND MEDIA

The post office is open Monday through Saturday 8:20 a.m.- 6:30 p.m. It closes at noon on the last day of the month. Stamps can be bought in *tabacchi* (tobacco shops) as well as in the post office. The *tabacchi,* as well as bars and some newsstands, also sell *gettoni* (L 200), tokens for use in telephones. *Schede telefòniche,* telephone cards are available for 5,000, 10,000 and 20,000 liras from *tabacchi* and newsstands.

The best way to make international calls is to use the card issued free by AT&T Direct Service. Ring the company's international operator who will connect you and add the charge to your bill back home. International calls can also be made from booths that accept credit cards. Collect calls can be made by ringing AT&T's international operator who will connect you at no charge.

In addition to the national newspapers, *La Republica*, *Il Corriere della Sera* and *L'Unità*, the Communist newspaper, one can purchase any of Sicily's own papers, *L'Ora* in Palermo, *La Sicilia* in Catania and *La Gazzetta del Sud* in Messina. For sports' fans there is the *Gazzetta dello Sport*. English-language newspapers are available in Palermo, Catania, Messina, Taormina and Cefalù. There are three state-run TV channels, *RAI, 1,2* and *3*, which have less advertising than the independent channels owned by Berlusconi. *RAI*'s radio stations are more professional than those run independently.

FESTIVALS

There are colorful festivals throughout the island at *Carnevale* (Carnival or Mardi Gras), the five days before Lent, sometime between the end of February and the beginning of March. Easter Week is a period of great festivity with processions and dramatic events. The biggest celebration throughout the island is at *ferragosto,* the Feast of the Assumption on August 15, with spectacular fireworks.

Other popular festivals are the Epiphany celebrations in Piana degli Albanesi (Jan.6), the Sant'Agata Feast in Catania (Feb.3-5), the celebration of The Almond Tree Blossoms in Agrigento (1st or 2nd week of Feb.). the Feast of Saint Rosalia in Palermo (July 11-15) and The Race of the Normans, a medieval-costumed procession and joust in Piazza Armerina (Aug. 13-14).

21

PUPPET THEATER

The puppet theater, which has been popular since the fourteenth century, is uniquely Sicilian. It depicts embellishments of the Charlemagne story, basically the battles between the Christians and the Saracen invaders. There is much clashing of swords and the piling up of bodies with large spurts of blood, with Orlando (Roland), Charlemagne's nephew, always the victor, be it in a fight with the infidel or with a crocodile.

THE SICILIAN DIALECT

Sicilian is truly not a dialect. Like Italian, it is a language derived directly from Latin. For political reasons, like 400 some-odd other tongues spoken throughout Italy, also derived from Latin, it is called a dialect. There can be only one official language of a country; all other idioms are relegated to the status of dialect.

Language is a mainstream of the life and culture of a people; it reflects its history, its manners and its very thoughts. Say <u>pasta cu sugu</u> (*pasta with a meat-tomato sauce*) and the Sicilian's soul-food leaps before your eyes, as do all the foods that enrich his table. Say <u>bonu com'u pani</u> (*as good as bread*) and you know that the Sicilian uses his crusty loaf as a yardstick to measure the value of all other things.

And, too, the dialect evokes his warm, intimate and loving family life, a family which has held his people together through 1500 years of invasions from greedy neighbors, the denuding of his land by the Arabian goat, the disappearance of his rich streams and luxuriant forests, the dessication of one of the richest lands in Europe, appreciated and loved by the early Greeks, who proudly named it Major Greece.

The same language tells you who occupied the island, used it and abused it — the early Greeks, the Romans, the Arabs, the Normans, the Byzantines, the French and the Spanish Bourbons. Look at the Sicilian names, some Greek in origin — mine, for example, Privitera, from *Presbitera*, the feminine of *Presbíteros*, elder, teacher, priest; some French, or Arabic — *sceccu* (SHEH koo), from Sheikh, a name given by the islanders to the donkey, in derision of their medieval Saracen masters, who rode on donkeys from village to village, maintaining order and collecting taxes.

23

Say *cíceri,* chickpeas (CHEE cheh ree) and the Sicilian Vespers leap to mind when, in the thirteenth century, the islanders rebelled against the French, their new oppressive masters. The Sicilians were able to identify them by their French pronunciation, (<u>SEE say ree</u>) of the word *cíceri.* Those who could not pronounce it correctly were put to the sword.

LANGUAGE LESSONS

25

PRONUNCIATION

VOWELS

Sicilian spelling of words (the orthography) is, like the Italian, fundamentally phonetic:**chiù**, *more*, **iddu**, *he,* **me patri**, *my father.* The stress falls on the next to the last syllable (penult): **parru**, *I speak.* Otherwise, stress is indicated by a bold, italicized vowel, **parranu**, *they speak.*

a, like *a* in 'father': as in **patri**, *father*, **matri**, *mother.*

e, like *e* in 'best': as in **bedda**, *beautiful.*

i, like *ea* as in 'beast': as in **kiddu**, *that, that one.*

ĭ, like *i* in 'fit': as in **fĭc ĭnu.** This short *i,* which appears in unstressed syllables, is not found in Italian.

o, like *aw in* 'claw': as in **tò, sò**, *your, yours, his, theirs*

u, almost like *o* in English 'to': as in **tuttu**, *all*, **unu**, *one.*

CONSONANTS

b,f,l,m,n,p,q,t,v   are pronounced as in English. Two consonants are written with two letters (digraphs),**ch** and **gh** .

c, before *e* or *i*, sounds like *ch* in 'choose,' as in **duci** , *sweet;* it is like English *k* before *a, o, u:* as in **cicara**, cup. It also has the *k* sound when it appears as **ch** before *e* or *i* as in **chi** , *what* or **checcu** , *stutterer.*

26

d, like *d* in Italian **do**, as in **dannu**, *harm*. But, at times, it will also sound like a sofly trilled *r*, both in initial position and between vowels; it is formed by the vibration of the tongue against the hard palate, as in **dumani**, *tomorrow*, **pedi**, *foot*. Double **dd** is soft when it appears between two vowels (intervocalic): as in **iddu**, *he*.

g, before *e* or *i*, sounds like *g* in 'George'; **gelu**, *frost*; **già**, *already*. It has the sound of *g* in 'gone' before *a, o, u*: as in **gattu**, *cat*, **goffu**, *stupid*, **gula**, *throat*. The digraph **gh** has the same hard sound before *e* or *i* : as in **gherciu**, *cross-eyed*, **ghiacciu**, *ice*.

h is always silent: as in **hannu**, *they have*.

i, unaccented, before a vowel, is pronounced like English *y*: as in **aiutu**, *help*; **chiù**, *more*. Also pronounced like English *y* when between two vowels (intervocalic), **vaiu**, *I go*.

n, before a **q**, a hard **c** (before, **a, o, u**) or **g** sounds like English *ng* (*wing*): as in **bancu** (BAHNG-ku), *bench*; **longu** (LONG-gu), *long*; **cinquanta** (ching-KWANTA), *fifty*.

r, when single, is formed with a quick flip of the tongue on the palate behind the front teeth: as in **caru**, *dear*; **puru**, *pure*. When **r** is double, or when it is the first letter in a word, the tongue is suspended between the roof and the bottom of the mouth, not touching either; its sides are curved against the sides of the mouth, while the tip is rounded to let the air escape as in **rota**, *wheel*; **carru**, *cart*.

s is pronounced like English s in 'soon,' but with a much sharper sound: as in **sulu**, *alone*; **spina**, *thorn*.
s before a sonant (**b,d,g,l,m,n,r,v**) sounds like English *z*; as in **sbirru**, *cop*; **sdegnu**, scorn; **sgranari**, *to shell*; **slitta**, *sleigh*;

27

smaltu, *enamel;* **s**nellu , *slender;* **s**radicari , *to uproot;* **s**veltu , *quick, alert.* Double s is pronounced like English *s* in 'see': as in chi**ss**u, *that one.*

u, unaccented, before a vowel, sounds like English *w*: as in **qu**annu (KWAHN-nu), *when;* **qu**attru, *four.*

z and **zz** are generally pronounced like a long and vigorous **ts**: as in **z**iu, *uncle,* pre**zz**u, *price.* In the following words, however, **z** and **zz** are pronounced like a prolonged **dz**; a**zz**urru, *blue,* du**zz**ina, *dozen,* men**z**u, *half.*

Note these combinations:

gghi , when followed by a consonant, is like English *g* in 'go': as in a**ggh**icari, *to arrive;* When followed by a vowel, it has a *g* (as in Eng. *go*) and *y* (a in Eng. *you*): as in a**gghi**u (AHG-you), *garlic;* fi**gghi**a, (FEEG-yah), *daughter.*

gn is like the *ni* in 'onion' as in o**gn**i, *every.*

qu, as in Italian, is always like *kw*: as in **qu**attru (KWAT-troo), *four;* **qu**innici (KWIN-nee-chee), *fifteen.*

sc before **e** and **i** is nearly like *sh* in 'ship'; as in **sc**iallu (SHALL-loo), *shawl;* **sc**emu (SHEH-moo)
In the **str** cluster, the t is not pronounced. The **s** and the **r** are pronounced together as air is forced through the slightly open teeth and lips, forming a sound close to the **sh** in Eng. *shame:* as in fine**str**a (feen NEsh rah), *window;* **str**ata (shRAH tah), *street.*

t, in the **nt** cluster, as in **nenti** , *nothing,* is pronounced as **d**, as in ne**nd**i.

The **tr** cluster is formed with the tip of the tongue touching the hard palate. The tongue is flat against the sides of the mouth to permit the simultaneous pronunciation of the **r**: as in **tri**, *three*.

In double consonants, both letters must be sounded, the first at the end of the preceding, the second at the beginning of the following syllable: **annu** (AHN noo), *year;* **chiddu** (KEED doo), *that.*

m, n and **r**, when preceded by an accented vowel and followed by another consonant, are prolonged: **sempri** (SEMM pree), *always;* **tantu** (TAHNN too), *so much;* **parti** (PAHRR tee), *part.*

Sicilian words are divided in such a way that, if possible, every syllable shall begin with a consonant: **men- zu**, *half;* **no- ta**, *note;* **nor- du**, *north.*

In the clusters noted above, **st, tr, gn, gghi,** the consonants belong to the following syllable. **fe- sta, o-gni, au-tru, a-gghiu.**

NB: Where indicated, we have used phonemic transcriptions to assist the reader in pronouncing a word or phrase correctly, e.g. **cascia** (KAH shah), *box.;* **quannu** (KWAHN noo), *when;* **picciriddu** (pitchi REE doo), *little boy.*

ABBREVIATIONS

adj	adjective	n	noun
adv	adverb	pl	plural
conj	conjunction	prep	preposition
def art	definite article	pret	preterite
indef art	indefinite article	pron	pronoun
f	feminine	sing	singular
m	masculine	vb	verb (infinitive)

LEZZIONI PRIMA ARRIVATA Ô ARIUPORTU

Ninu e Maria Mondello, figghi di Siciliani nasciuti in America, arrivanu a Roma da Nova York.

Ninu: U sai, Maria, chi u nomi di stu ariuportu è Leonardo da Vinci, ma tutti u chiamanu Fiumicinu.

Maria: U sacciu... Talia, ora bisogna prisintari i passaporti.

Ninu: U Consulatu Italianu a Nova York mi dissi chi nun c'è chiù bisognu di vistu nu passaportu.

Ninu porgi i so passaporti ô ufficiali cu li stampa. Nâ dugana c' è una linia pî turisti che hannu qualchi cosa a dichiarari e un autra pi chiddi chi nun hannu nenti a dichiarari.

Ninu: *Ô ufficiali.* Nun havemu nenti a dichiarari.

L'Ufficiali : Putiti passari.

Ninu : Scusatimi, ma unna iemu pi pigghiari l'ariuplanu â Sicilia?

L'Ufficiali : Iti â destra pi truvari l'ALITALIA.

Ninu : Grazii. Iamu, Maria.

Maria: Ninu, ddocu è l'ALITALIA.

Ninu : Scusatimi. Quannu è u prossimu volu a Palermo?

U Rapprisintanti: Fra un ura. Vi prenutu dui posti.

LESSON ONE ARRIVAL AT THE AIRPORT

Ninu and Maria Mondello, offspring of Sicilians, born in America, arrive at Rome from New York.

Ninu: Maria, you know, don't you, that this airport is called the Leonardo da Vinci, but that everyone calls it Fiumicino.

Maria: I know, but look, we have to present our passports.

Ninu: I was told by the Italian Consulate in New York that it is no longer necessary to have a visa.

Ninu hands their passports to the officer, who stamps them. At Customs there is a line for tourists who have something to declare and another for those who have nothing to declare.

Ninu : *To the Officer* We have nothing to declare.

The Officer : You may pass.

Ninu : Excuse me, but where do we go to catch the plane to Sicily?

L'Ufficiali : Off to the right you'll find ALITALIA.

Ninu : Thank you. Let's go, Maria.

Maria: Ninu, there's ALITALIA.

Ninu : Excuse me. When is the next flight to Palermo?

The Agent: In an hour. I'll reserve two seats for you.

VOCABULARY

â	to the
ariuportu	airport
arrivanu	they arrive
arrivata	arrival
autra	other
bisogna	it is necessary to
c'è	there is
chi	what, that
chiamanu	they call
chiddu	that, that of
chiddi	those
chiù	more, anymore
ci	there
Consulatu Italianu	Italian Consulate
coppia	couple
cosa	thing
cu	who
da	from
destra	right (side)
di	of
dichiarari	to declare
dissi	told
ddocu	there
dugana	customs
dui	two
e	and
è	is
faci	he, she makes
figghi	children
fra	within
grazzii	thanks

hannu	they have
havemu	we have
iamu	let us go
iemu	we go
in	in
iri	to go
iti	go
lezzioni	lesson
li	them
linii	lines
ma	but
mi	me
nasciuti	born
nenti	nothing
nomi	name
Nova York	New York
nu	in the
nun	not
ora	now
ô	to the
passaporti	passports
passari	pass
pi	to, in order to
pî	for the
pigghiari	get, catch
porgi	he hands, gives
posti	seats
prenutu	I (will) reserve
prima	first
prisintari	to present
prossimu, u	the next
putiti	you can, may
qualchi	some

quannu	when
rapprisintanti	agent
sacciu	I know
sai	you know
scus*a*timi	excuse me
so	his
stampa	stamps
stu	this
sunu	they are
tal*i*a	look
truvari	to find
turisti	tourists
tutti	everyone
u	it, the
ufficiali	officer
una	one
unna	where
ura	hour
vi	to, for you,
vistu	visa
volu	flight

LOCUZIONI

EXPRESSIONS

figghi di Siciliani	children of Sicilians
chiamanu stu ariuportu Fiumicinu	they call this airport Fiumicinu
tal*i*a	look
bisogna prisintari i passaporti	we have to present our passports
nun c'è chiù bisognu di vistu	visas are no longer needed
nun havemu nenti a dichiarari	we have nothing to declare
putiti passari	you may pass
unna iemu pi pigghiari l'ariuplanu	where do we go to catch the

â Sicilia?	plane to Sicily?
iti â destra	go to the right
iamu, Maria	let's go, Maria
quannu è u prossimu volu?	when is the next flight?
fra un ura	in one hour
vi prenutu dui posti	I'll reserve two seats for you

ESERCIZI

EXERCISES

1. Copy the text, read it aloud and translate it.

2. Translate into Sicilian:
Where do we go to catch the plane to Sicily? In an hour.
When is the next flight? Go to the right

3. Translate into English:
Talìa. Vi prenutu dui posti. Iamu, Maria. Scusatimi.

4. Memorize the following:

vi prenutu dui posti	I'll reserve two seats for you
iti â destra	go to the right
nun havemu nenti a dichiarari	we have nothing to declare
talìa	look

GRAMMAR

I. Articles

The article agrees with its noun in gender and number.

A. The Definite Article

Masculine

Singular, **u**

u patri, *the father*
u figghiu, *the son*

Plural, **i**

i patri, *the fathers*
i figghi, *the sons*

Feminine

Singular, **a**

a f*i*mmina, *the woman*
a matri, *the mother*

Plural, **i**

i f*i*mmini, *the women*
i matri, *the mothers*

Before a vowel, Masculine or Feminine

l'

l'occhiu, *the eye*
l'angilu, *the angel*
l'acula, *the eagle*

li

li occhi, *the eyes*
li angili, *the angels*
li aculi, *the eagles*

36

B. The Indefinite Article

Masculine

(a) **U n** before a vowel or any consonant excepts + consonant or **z**.

    un aneddu, *a ring*   **un** patri, *a father*

(b) **U nu** before **s** + consonant or **z**

    unu specchiu, *a mirror*   **unu** ziu, *an uncle*

Feminine

Una   **un'** before a vowel.

una matri, *a mother*   **un'** ura, *an hour*

The indefinite article is omitted in Sicilian before a predicate noun (a noun used with the verb *to be*), expressing occupation, condition, rank, or nationality, but not modified by an adjective.

    È pueta, *he is a poet*.   Sunu italiani, *they are Italians*.
          È medicu, *he is a doctor*.

But it is used when the noun is modified by an adjective:

    È **un** bonu medicu, *he is a good doctor*.

ESERCIZI: Translate the following into Sicilian:

1. Ninu Mondello is a doctor. 2. Anna Mondello is a professor of English. 3. Gianni is a good poet.

LEZZIONI SECUNNA   PRISINTAZZIONI

Dui coppii, arrivati a Roma da Nova York, si canuscianu ntô ariuplanu chi va da Roma â Sicilia. Ninu e Maria Mondello, Gianni e Anna Orlando.

Ninu: Permettitimi di prisintarmi. Mi chiamu Ninu Mondello e chista è me sposa, Maria Mondello.

Gianni: Contentu di canuscirivi. Iu mi chiamu Gianni Orlando e chista è me sposa Anna Orlando.Parrati sicilianu accussì bonu chi forsi vuautri puru siti Siciliani.

Ninu: U fattu è chi nascemmu in America, figghi di Siciliani.

Maria: E sempri avemu parratu in dialettu.

Anna: Voli diri chi aviti sempri parratu Sicilianu e Inglisi.

Ninu: È propriu accussì. E vuautri, siti Siciliani?

Gianni: Sì; ma avemu visitatu parenti in America e ora stamu riturnannu a San Fratello,u nostru paisi, unna semu tutti i dui prufissuri di francisi. E vuautri chi siti?

Ninu: Iu sugnu medicu, e me mugghieri è prufissuri di inglisi.

Gianni: Sintiti. Cca c'è u me numiru di telefonu. Si putiti veniri a San Fratello, chiamatimi e viniti passari unu o dui iorna cu nuautri.

Ninu: Cu piaciri. Milli grazii.

LESSON TWO   INTRODUCTIONS

Two couples, having arrived at Rome from New York, meet on the plane to Sicily. Ninu and Maria Mondello, Gianni and Anna Orlando.

Ninu: Allow me to introduce myself. I am Ninu Mondello and this is my wife, Maria Mondello.

Gianni: Glad to meet you. I am Gianni Orlando and this is my wife, Anna Orlando. I thought you were American, but you speak Sicilian so well that perhaps you, too, are Sicilian.

Ninu: The fact is we were born in America of Sicilian parents.

Maria: And we have always spoken the dialect.

Anna: So you have always spoken Sicilian and English.

Ninu: That's right. Are you Sicilians?

Gianni: Yes; but we have been visiting relatives in the States and we are now returning home to San Fratello, where we both teach French. And what is your profession?

Ninu: I am a doctor and my wife teaches English.

Gianni: Look; here is my telephone number. Call me if you can come to San Fratello to spend a couple of days with us.

Ninu: With pleasure, and many thanks.

VOCABULARY

a	to
accussì bonu	so well
avemu parratu	we have spoken
avemu visitatu	we have visited
cca	here
c'è	is
chi	that,what
chiamatimi	call me
coppii	couples
cuntenti di canuscirivi	glad to meet you
cu	with
da	of, from
dialettu	dialect
dui	two
è propriu accussì	that's right
figghi	sons, children
forsi	perhaps
francisi	French
grazii	thanks
in	in
inglisi	English
iornu, iorna	day, days
Iu	I
ma	but
me	my
medicu	doctor
mi chiamu	my name is
milli	a thousand
mugghieri	wife
nascemmu	we were born
numiru	number

nuautri	we, us
o	or
ora	now
paisi	town
parenti	relatives
parrati	you speak
passari	pass, spend
pensavu chi fussivu	I thought you were
permettitimi di prisintarmi	may I introduce myself
piaciri	pleasure
prufissuri	professor, teacher
putiti	you can
puru	also, too
se	if
sempri	always
semu	we are
sì	yes
Siciliani	Sicilians
sintiti	listen
siti	you are
sposa	wife
stamu riturnannu	we are returning
sugnu	I am
telefonu	telephone
tutti i dui	the two of us
u fattu è	the fact is
unu	one
unna	where
u nostru	our
veniri	(to) come
viniti	(you) come
voli diri	it means, that's saying
vuautri	you

LOCUZIONI

permettitimi di prisintarmi
mi chiamu
cuntenti di canuscirivi
u fattu è
voli diri
è propriu accussì
u nostru paisi
e vuautri chi siti?
cà c'è
u me numiru di telefonu
viniti passari
cu piaciri
milli grazii

EXPRESSIONS

allow me to introduce myself
my name is
glad to meet you
the fact is
that means
that's it, exactly
our hometown
and what do you do?
here is
my telephone number
come and spend
with pleasure
many thanks

ESERCIZI

EXERCISES

1. Copy the text, read it aloud and translate it.

2. Make up sentences with the following phrases and repeat them three times:
Mi chiamu. Cuntenti di canuscirivi. U nostru paisi.

3. Translate into Sicilian:
Allow me to introduce myself. We were born in America. Many thanks. Are you Sicilians?

4. Translate into English:
Cà c'è u me numiru di telefonu. Avemu visitatu parenti in America. Viniti passare unu o dui iorna cu nuautri. Cuntenti di canuscirivi.

5. Memorize the names Ninu, Maria, Gianni, Anna.

GRAMMAR

II.Nouns

A.Gender

(a)<u>Masculine</u> — those ending in -u: u dinocchiu, *the knee;*
u figghiu, *the son*

(Some exceptions: a manu, *the hand;* a virtù, *the virtue,*
a soru, *the sister;* a ficu, *the fig)*

(b)<u>Feminine</u> —those ending in -a: a figghia, *the daughter*
(Some exceptions: u telegramma, *the telegram,* u sofà,
the sofa)
—those ending in -zioni , -giuni : l' azioni , *the*
action; a priggiuni , *the prison;* a ragiuni , *the reason*

(c)<u>Masculine or Feminine</u> — a few, ending in -i can be either
u patri, *the father*   u frati, *the brother*
a matri, *the mother*   a vutti, *the barrel*

B.Number

<u>Masculine nouns,</u>whatever the ending, form their plural in -i

u pueta, *the poet*   i pueti, *the poets*
u medicu, *the doctor*   i medici, *the doctors*
u frati, *the brother*   i frati, the *brothers*

(a)Masculines ending in -ca or -cu and -ga or -gu add an h before
the plural ending, in order to retain the original hard sound of the
consonant, chi (kee) and -ghi (ghee) respectively.

43

u monarca, *the monarch*	i monarchi, *the monarchs*
l'anticu, *ancient*	li antichi, *the ancients*
u collega, *the colleague*	i colleghi, *the colleagues*
u lagu, *the lake*	i laghi, *the lakes*

<u>(Some exceptions:</u>

-cu > -ci

medicu, *the doctor,* medici; amicu, *friend,* amici;
grecu, *Greek,* greci; nemicu, *enemy,* nemici; porcu, *pig,*
porci

(b) The following masculines, which end in -u, have an irregular
feminine plural in -a:

cintinaru, *hundred*	cintinara, *hundreds*
migghiu, *mile*	migghia, *miles*
migghiaru, *thousand*	migghiara, *thousands*
paru, *pair*	para, *pairs*
ovu, *egg*	ova, *eggs*

<u>Feminine nouns,</u> whatever the ending, form their plural in -i.

a strata, *the street*	i strati, *the streets*
a matri, *the mother*	i matri, *the mothers*
a guancia *the cheek*	i guanci, *the cheeks*

(a) Feminines ending in -ca or -cu add an **h** before the plural
ending, in order to retain the original hard sound of the consonant,
— **chi** (kee) and -**ghi** (ghee) respectively.

| un' oca, *a goose* | tri ochi, *three geese* |
| a fuga, *the flight* | i fughi, *the flights* |

44

<u>Invariables</u> - these are nouns which retain the same ending in the plural:

all monosyllables: u re, *the king* - i re, *the kings*

all nouns ending in:
— i - u brindisi, *the toast* - i brindisi, *the toasts*
        a matri, *the mother* - i matri, *the mothers*
— an accented vowel: una cità, *a city* - tri cità, *three cities*
— a consonant: l'onnibus, *the bus* - li onnibus, *the buses*

ESERCIZI: Translate the following into Sicilian:

1. A pair of eggs. 2. Ninu and Gianni are friends. 3.Hundreds of miles. 4.The doctors are not Sicilians; they are Greek. 5. The brothers are colleagues.

LEZZIONI TERZA   IN TASSÍ-E IN AUTOBUS

Ninu: Ora chi arrivammu a Palermo, bisogna pigghiari un tassí pir iri a l'albergu.

Maria: Comu si chiama u nostru albergu?

Ninu: U Pretoria... Tassista, quantu custa a cursa ô Pretoria?

Tassista: Sissanta mila liri.

Ninu: Benissimu. Eccu i nostri valiggi. Iamu.

Maria: Ninu, nun è veru chi u Pretoria è un albergu discretu e vicinu â Via Maqueda?

Ninu: È veru. A Maqueda è na via centrali di Palermo.

....
Maria: Ora chi havemu na bedda stanza cu duccia, putemu ripusari.

Ninu: Si, e dumani putemu fari un giru di Palermo in autobus.

....
Maria: Ora chi havemu fattu culazioni, putemu accuminciari u giru.

Ninu: Maria, oggi putemu usari i biglietti chi accattammu ieri pi quattru mila liri ciascunu. Cu sti biglietti putemu viaggiari tutta a iornata ntâ cità.

Maria: Oggi vulissi visitari i punti chiù interessanti di Palermo.

Ninu: Ma certu. Pi lu menu San Giovanni degli Eremiti, u Palazzu dî Normanni e a Vucciria unni si pò accattari qualsiasi tipu di mangiari.

46

LESSON THREE   BY TAXI AND BUS

Ninu: Now that we've arrived in Palermo, we must catch a cab to get to our hotel.

Maria: What's the name of our hotel?

Ninu : The Pretoria... Driver, how much does it cost to the Pretoria?

Cabdriver: Sixty thousand liras.

Ninu : Fine. Here are our valises. Let us go.

Maria: Ninu, isn't it true that the Pretoria is a modestly priced hotel and that it is near the Via Maqueda?

Ninu: That's right. The Maqueda is a main Palermo road.
....
Maria: Now that we have a nice room with shower,we can rest.

Ninu: Yes, and tomorrow we can tour Palermo by bus.
....
Maria: Now that we have had breakfast, we can begin our tour.

Ninu: Maria, today we can use the tickets we bought yesterday for four thousand liras apiece. With these tickets we can travel throughout the city all day.

Maria: Today I'd like to visit Palermo's most interesting spots.

Ninu: Of course. San Giovanni degli Eremiti,The Norman Palace and the Vucciria, where one can buy any kind of food.

VOCABULARY

â	to the
accattammu	we bought
accattari	buy, to buy
albergu	hotel
arrivammu	we arrived
*au*tobus	bus
bedda	beautiful
ben*i*ssimu	fine
biglietti	tickets
bisogna pigghiari	we must take
centrali	central, main
certu	of course
chiù	more
ciascunu	each
città	city
comu	how, what
culazioni	breakfast
accuminciari	begin
cursa	(taxi) run
cu	with
custa	costs
di	of
discretu	modest
duccia	shower
dumani	tomorrow
eccu	here is, are
fari	do, to do
giru	tour
havemu	we have
fattu	done, had
ieri	yesterday

in	in, by
interessanti	interesting
iornata	day
iri	to go
liri	liras
ma	but
mangiari	food
mila	thousand
na	a
nostru	our
ntâ	in the
nun	not
ô	to the
oggi	today
ora	now
pi, pir	for, to
pi lu menu	at least
punti	places
putemu	we can
qualsiasi	any
quantu	how much
quattru	four
ripusari	rest, to rest
sì	yes
si chiama	is called
si pò	one can
sissanta	sixty
stanza	room
tassí	taxi
tassista	driver
tipu	type, kind
tutta	all
unni	where

usari	use, to use
valigi	valises
veru	true
via	road
viaggiari	travel
vicinu	near
visitari	visit, to visit
vulissi	I would want

LOCUZIONI

EXPRESSIONS

bisogna pigghiari un tassí	we (one) must get a taxi
comu si chiama	what is the name of
quantu custa	what is the cost of
ben*i*ssimu	fine, very well
eccu i nostri valiggi	here are our valises
nun è veru chi?	isn't it true that
na bedda stanza cu duccia	a beautiful room with shower
putemu ripusari	we can rest
un albergu discretu	a modestly priced hotel
fari un giru	tour
havemu fattu culazioni	we have had breakfast
putemu viaggiari	we can travel
tutta a iornata	all day long
ntâ cità	through the city
i punti chiù interessanti	the more interesting places
qualsiasi tipu di mangiari	any type of food

ESERCIZI   EXERCISES

1. Copy the text, read it aloud and translate it.

2. Make up sentences with the following phrases and repeat them
three times:
fari un giru; quantu custa; tutta a iornata; un albergu discretu

3. Translate into Sicilian:
One can buy almost any kind of food in the Vucciria.Tomorrow we
can tour Palermo by bus. What's the name of our hotel?

4. Translate into English:
Nun è veru chi u Pretoria è un albergu discretu? Havemu na bedda
stanza cu duccia. Oggi putemu usari i biglietti chi accattammu ieri.

5. Memorize:
qualsiasi tipu di mangiari; cu sti biglietti putemu viaggiari
tutta a iornata; fari un giru; na bedda stanza cu duccia.

GRAMMAR

III.Adjectives

Adjectives agree with their nouns in gender and number.

U gattu è pulitu   *The cat is neat*
Stanzi puliti   *Neat rooms*
A picciridda è bedda   *The little girl is pretty*

A.Gender and Number

Adjectives which end in - **u** are masculine and form their feminine in
-**a**. Adjectives which end in- **i** are invariable and have the same
ending in the masculine and feminine.

bonu libbru, *good book*   bona scarpa, *good shoe*
picciotu felici, *happy boy*   picciotta felici, *happy girl*

Adjectives form their plural in the same way as nouns:
Masc.- **u** to -i   Fem.-**a** to -**i**   -**i** to - **i**

un figghiu bonu *a good son*   i figghi boni *the good sons*
na picciotta bona *a good girl*   i picciotti boni, *the good girls*
un patri bonu, *a good father*   dui patri boni, *two good fathers*

Adjectives of either gender or number may be used as a noun
     i boni, *the good.*   **a bella**, *the beautiful woman*

B. Comparison

(a) All Sicilian adjectives form

— their comparative by prefixing **chiù**, *more*, to the adjective
        chiù beddu, *more beautiful*
        chiù longu, *longer*
— their superlative, by prefixing the definite article (u̲, a̲) to the comparative.

      u chiù beddu, *the most beautiful*
      u chiù longu, *the longest*

(b) When the superlative immediately follows the noun, the definite article is omitted
      a vía **chiù** curta, *the shortest way*

(c) Two adjectives have an irregular comparison in addition to the regular one, megghiu, *better,* and peggiu, *worse.*

      chiù bonu(a) or megghiu, *better*
      u (a) **chiù** bonu(a) or u̲ (a̲) megghiu, *the best*
      chiù malu(a) or peggiu, *worse*
      u (a)**chiù** malu(a) or u̲ (a̲) peggiu, the worst

A casa di Iachinu è **chiù** bona (megghiu) da mia.
Jack's house is better than mine.
A casa di Iachinu è **chiù** mala (peggiu) da mia
Jack's house is worse than mine.
A casa di Iachinu è **a chiù** bona (a̲ megghiu)
Jack's house is the best.
A casa di Iachinu è **a chiù** mala (a̲ peggiu)
Jack's house is the worst.

53

(d) *Larger* and *smaller* (size) are **chiù** granni and **chiù** nicu;
Older and *younger* (age) are **maggiuri** and **minuri**

A casa di Ninu è a **chiù** granni.	*Nino's house is the largest.*
Paulu è u frati **chiù** nicu.	*Paul is the smallest brother.*
Ninu è u frati **minuri**.	*Nino is the youngest brother.*

(e) The adverb *less* is expressed by **menu**; *least* by **u(a) menu**
Sta stanza è **a menu** bella.   *This room is the least pretty.*

(f) *Than* is **chi**
              L'albergu è chiù granni **chi** bellu.
              The hotel is larger than it is beautiful.
— But before a noun, a pronoun, or a numeral, *than* is rendered by
the preposition **di**.
              Iddi sunnu chiù ricchi **du** re.   *They are richer than the king.*
              Filippu è pegghiu **di** mia.   *Philip is worse than I.*
              Menu **di** cincu.   *Less than five.*

(g) *The more...the more* is **chiù ...chiù**.
      Chiù studiu **chiù** imparu.   *The more I study the more I learn.*

—*The less...the less* is **menu ...menu**.
      Menu studiu **menu** imparu. *The less I study the less I learn.*

ESERCIZI: Translate the following into Sicilian:

1. Paul is the oldest brother. 2. Ninu is smaller than Paul.
3. This room is the largest.

54

LEZZIONI QUARTA   L'ALBERGU

Ninu: Sta prima culazioni chi l'albergu ni offri ntâ sala da pranzu è differenti da nostra culazionai in America.

Maria: È veru; cca ni dunanu pani e burru e cunserva di frutta e caffè e latti.

Ninu: Si, ma dumani vogghiu pruvari u bar cca vicinu unna putemu aviri una spremuta di aranci, un cappuccinu e cornettu.

Maria: Una bona idea, Ninu. Allura facemu accussì.

Ninu: U nostru lettu è commudu ma nun ti pari strana a stanza du bagnu cu sulu a duccia?

Maria: Strana daveru. Iu prefirisciu lavarmi na vasca du bagnu, inveci dâ duccia.

Ninu: E iu prefirisciu a duccia.

Maria: Quantu ni fannu pagari pâ stanza?

Ninu: Sissanta mila liri. Nun ti pari un prezzu discretu?

Maria: Si, daveru. Dimmi, Ninu, quannu ni riturnanu i passaporti?

Ninu: Oggi, dissi l'albergaturi.

Maria: Benissimu. Allura, continuamu u giru di Palermo.

Ninu: Si; ma oggi u giru è a pedi.

55

LESSON FOUR   THE HOTEL

Ninu: This first breakfast which the hotel is serving us in the dining room is quite different than ours in the States.

Maria: That's true; here they give us bread and butter and fruit preserves and coffee and milk.

Ninu: Yes, but tomorrow I want to try the nearby bar, where we can have freshly squeezed orange juice, a cappuccino and a *cornetto*, that's a chocolate- or custard-filled croissant.

Maria: A good idea, Ninu. Let's do just that.

Ninu: Our bed is comfortable but don't you think our bathroom feels strange with only a shower?

Maria: Strange, indeed.I prefer to bathe in a bathtub instead of the shower.

Ninu: I prefer the shower.

Maria: How much are we paying for our room?

Ninu: Sixty thousand liras. Don't you think that's reasonable?

Maria: Yes, indeed. Tell me, when will they return our passports?

Ninu: The hotelier said, today.

Maria: Fine. Now let's continue our tour of Palermo.

Ninu: Yes; but today it will be on foot.

VOCABULARY

albergaturi	hotelier
albergu	hotel
allura	then
aranci	oranges
aviri	have, to have
bar	coffee shop
benissimu	fine
bon', bonu,-a	good
burru	butter
caffè	coffee
cappuccinu	cappuccino
cca	here
commudu	comfortable
continuamu	we continue
cornettu	filled croissant
cunserva di frutta	fruit preserves
daveru	indeed, really
differenti	different
dimmi	tell me
discretu	reasonable
dissi	he, she said
duccia	shower
dunanu	they give
quantu	they make, do
facemu	we do, let's do
idea	idea
inveci di	instead of
iu	I
latti	milk
lavarmi	to wash myself
lettu	bed

57

ma	but
mila	thousand
ni	us
ntâ	in the
offri	offers
oggi	today
pâ	for the
pagari	pay, to pay
pani	bread
pari	seem
passaporti	passports
pedi, a	on foot
prima culazioni	breakfast
prefirisciu	I prefer
prezzu	price
pruvari	to try
putemu	we can
quannu	when
quantu	how much
riturnanu	they return
sala da pranzu	dining room
sissanta	sixty
stanza du bagnu	bathroom
sta	this
stanza	room
spremuta	squeezed juice
strana	strange
ti	to you
sulu	only
vasca du bagnu	bathtub
vicinu	near

LOCUZIONI	EXPRESSIONS
prima culazioni	breakfast
sala da pranzu	dining room
cunserva di frutta	fruit preserves
vogghiu pruvari	I want to try
cca vicinu	nearby
spremuta di aranci	freshly squeezed orange juice
una bona idea	a good idea
facemu accussì	let's do just that
a stanza du bagnu	the bathroom
strana, daveru	strange, indeed
a vasca du bagnu	the bathtub
quantu ni fannu pagari	how much do we have to pay
un prezzu discretu	a reasonable price
sì, daveru	yes, indeed
u giru è a pedi	the tour is on foot

ESERCIZI

EXERCISES

1. Copy the text, read it aloud and translate it.

2. Make up sentences with the following phrases and repeat them three times:
fari un giru a pedi; sì, daveru; prefirisciu a duccia; un prezzu discretu

3. Translate into Sicilian:
our bed is comfortable; I want to try the nearby bar; today the tour will be on foot; I prefer to bathe in a bathtub

4. Translate into English:
nun ti pari un prezzu discretu? iu prefirisciu lavarmi na vasca du bagnu; iu prefirisciu a duccia; allura facemu accussì

5. Memorize:
continuamu u giru di Palermo; u nostru lettu è comudu; putemu haviri una spremuta di aranci; quantu ni fannu pagari pâ stanza?

GRAMMAR
IV. Augmentatives & Diminutives

Sicilian often uses a suffix to express size or quality. The suffix may be added to a noun, an adjective or an adverb.

Augmentatives

(a) The commonest ending is *-íssimu* (fem.*-íssima*), *very*, which in general is added only to adjectives and adverbs.

> largu, (adj)*wide*   largh*íssimu* , *very wide*
> granni,(adj) *big*   grann*íssimu* , *very big*
> beni, (adv) *well*   ben*íssimu* , *very well*

(b) The **-azzu (-a)** and **-uni** suffixes denote bigness, but usually in a pejorative sense.

> Havi una bucc**azza**   *She has a big mouth.*
> U chiamanu man**azza** .   *They call him B ig Hands (because he has large hands).*
> **Nasuni**   *Bignose*

Diminutives

Sicilians love diminutives, which they use to express not only size but feeling and affection. Sicilian has basically only four:

- **uzzu** (-a); - **ceddu** (-a); -**iddu** (a); and - **inu**

(a) - **uzzu** denotes affection. It is an exclusive Sicilian term of endearment extended not only to people but to things as well.

u pan**uzzu-** *the bread, i.e. the wonderful, sweet, lovely bread*
Pippin**uzzu** - *little Pippinu, our dear Pippinu*

It has been so widely used that it has worked its way into proper names, as in **Maruzza**, a diminutive of *Maria*, which, however, does not indicate smallness.

(b) - **ceddu** (-a) denotes smallness, also "somewhat, something of"

a casi**cedda**	*the small house*
é brutt**icedda**	*she's somewhat ugly, not really pretty*
é latr**iceddu**	*he's something of a thief*

(c)-**iddu**. The best known example of this suffix is found in *Tur<u>iddu</u>*, the diminutive of Salvaturi - Salva**turiddu**.

(d)- **inu** (-a) **buccuncinu**, *a "sweet" mouthful*. It is used as the name of a cream puff filled with sweet ricotta.

62

ESERCIZI: Translate the following into Sicilian:

1. They call Paul bighands. 2.The room is very wide.
3. Pippinuzzu is Turiddu's brother.

LEZZIONI QUINTA

DUMMANARI DIREZIONI

Ninu: Maria, sta spremuta di aranci è frisca e sapurita.

Maria: D'accordu. E u cappuccinu è deliziusu. Ora putemu accumminciari u giru a pedi, nun è veru?

Ninu: Si, ma prima bisogna dummanari direzioni. *Ô impiegatu dô bar*. Susatimi, stamu facennu un giru dâ cità a pedi; mi pò diri comu putemu iri ô Corso Vittorio Emanuele?

L'Impiegatu: È facili; l'albergu è nâ Via Maqueda. Iti â sinistra e a prinicpali strata chi incontrati è u Corso.

Ninu: Grazii. Iamu, Maria. A carta stratali *i*ndica chi l'Università è prâ via; e pocu doppu di dari un'ucchiata â sedi intellettuali di Palermo, arrivamu ô CorsoVittorio Emanuele.

Maria: Ora chi l'havemu vistu, e chi havemu passatu a Piazza Bellini, chiamata accussì in onuri dû gran composituri sicilianu, arrivammu ê Quattru Canti, unna si cr*u*cianu o Corso e a Via Maqueda.

Ninu: Si, è un puntu anticu di Palermo, criatu in 1611. In ogni cantu c'è una statua.

Maria: Nínu, ora sugnu stanca e haiu fami. Pirchì nun pigghiamu un autobus finu â Vucciria?

Ninu: Si, e dda putemu truvari un picculu ristoranti unna putemu mangiari carni o pisci frischi. Iamu.

LESSON FIVE   ASKING FOR DIRECTIONS

Ninu: Maria, this freshly squeezed orange juice is fresh and tasty.

Maria: I agree, and the cappuccino is delicious. Now we can start our tour on foot, can't we?

Ninu: Yes, but first we must ask for directions. *To the bar attendant.* Excuse me, we're touring the city on foot; can you tell me how to get to the Corso Vittorio Emanuele?

The Attendant: That's easy; the hotel is on the Via Maqueda. Go left and the first principal street you encounter is the Corso.

Ninu: Thanks. Let's go, Maria. The street map indicates that the University is on the way; and shortly after looking over Palermo's intellectual seat, we'll arrive at the Corso.

Maria: Now that we have seen it and that we have passed the Piazza Bellini, named in honor of the great Sicilian composer, we've arrived at the Quattru Canti, The Four Corners, where the Corso and the Via Maqueda meet.

Ninu: Yes, it's one of Palermo's oldest spots, created in 1611. There's a statue in every corner.

Maria: Ninu, now I'm tired and hungry. Why don't we take a bus up to the Vucciria?

Ninu: Yes, and there we can find a small restaurant where we can eat meat or fresh fish. Let's go.

VOCABULARY

accumminciari	to begin
anticu	old, ancient
bisogna	one must
cantu	corner
cappuccinu	cappuccino
carni	meat
carta	map
chiamata	called
composituri	composer
comu	how
criatu	created
crucianu	they cross
dari	to give
deliziusu	delicious
doppu	after
dummanari	to ask for
facili	easy
fami	hungry, hunger
finu a	up to
frisca	fresh
gran	great
haiu	I have, am
impiegatu	employee
incontrati	you encounter
indica	indicates
intellettuali	intellectual
iri	to go
iti	you go
mangiari	to eat
o	or
ogni	every

66

onuri	honor
passatu	passed
p*i*cculu	small
pigghiamu	we take
pisci	fish
pocu	a little
pri	on
prima	first
principali	principal
puntu	point, location
putemu	we can
ristoranti	restaurant
sapurita	tasty
sedi	seat
sinistra	the left
sugnu	I am
stamu facennu	we are doing
stanca	tired
statua	statue
strata	street
stratali	street, *adj*
truvari	find
ucchiata	glance
università	university
unna [unni]	where
via	the way
vistu	seen

LOCUZIONI

EXPRESSIONS

d'accordu	agreed, I agree
nun è veru?	isn't it so (true)?

bisogna dummanari direzioni	we must ask for directions
mi pò diri?	can you tell me?
è facili	that's easy
iti â sinistra	go to the left
a carta stratali	the street map
dari un'ucchiata	give a glance
chiamata accussì	so called
è un puntu anticu	it's an old spot
sugnu stanca	I am tired
haiu fami	I am hungry
un *au*tobus finu â Vucciria	a bus up to the Vucciria
ddà putemu truvari	there we can find
mangiari carni o pisci frischi	eat meat or fresh fish

ESERCIZI

EXERCISES

1. Copy the text, read it aloud and translate it.

2. Make up sentences with the following phrases and repeat them three times:
iti â sinistra; sugnu stancu; haiu fami; nun è veru?;

3. Translate into Sicilian:
there we can eat fresh fish; go to the left; there we can find a restaurant; where is the university?

4. Translate into English:
ma prima bisogna dummanari direzioni; mi pò diri comu putemu iri ô Corso Vittorio Emanuele?; in ogni cantu c'è una statua; sugnu stanca e haiu fami

5. Memorize:
haiu fami; sugnu stancu; iti â sinistra; unni è a Vucciria?

GRAMMAR

V. Numerals

The Cardinals

1 unu	11 *u*nnici	30 trenta
2 dui	12 d*u*dici	40 quaranta
3 tri	13 tr*i*dici	50 cinquanta
4 quattru	14 quatt*o*rdici	60 sissanta
5 cincu	15 qu*i*nnici	70 sittanta
6 sei	16 s*i*dici	80 ottanta
7 setti	17 dicisetti	90 novanta
8 ottu	18 diciottu	100 centu
9 novi	19 dicinovi	200 ducentu
10 deci	20 vinti	300 tricentu

1,000 milli — 2,000 dumila — 1,000,000 un miliuni

Unu has a feminine, una; when used as an adjective, it has the same forms as the indefinite article.

una cosa, *one thing*

The plural of milli is mila as in dumila .

dumila casi, *two thousand houses*

1.Unlike English,
no conjunction is used between the different parts of a number
—**ducentu quaranta** , *two hundred <u>and</u> forty;*

69

nor is an indefinite article used before **centu** and **milli**
—**centu libri** , _a hundred books_, **milli scuti** , _a thousand dollars_

2. _Both, all three,_ etc. are **tutti i dui, tutti i tri**, etc.

3. _What time is it?_ is **chi ura è ?** or **chi ura sunu ?** _It is six_, etc.,
is **sunu i sei** , etc. **ura** being understood.

Sunu i dui e menzu.	_It is half past two._
Sunu i tri e deci.	_It is ten minutes past three._
Ci mancanu vinti minuti pî quattru	_It is twenty minute to four._
Sunu i cincu menu un quartu.	_It is a quarter to five._

The Ordinals

1st	**primu**	8th	**ottavu**
2d	**secunnu**	9th	**nonu**
3d	**terzu**	10th	**decimu**
4th	**quartu**	20th	**vintesimu**
5th	**quintu**	30th	**trentesimu**
6th	**sestu**	100th	**centesimu**
7th	**settimu**	1,000th	**millesimu**

All ordinals form their feminines and plurals like other adjectives
which end in **- u**

a terza figghia si chiama Carla, _the third daughter is called Carla_
   chista è a quinta lezzioni, _this is the fifth lesson_

70

(a) Ordinal numerals are used after the names of rulers, without the article.

Carlu **Secunnu**   *Charles the Second*
Piu **Nonu**   *Pius IX*

(b) For the day of the month, except the first, a cardinal number is used.

cincu d'aprili.   *The fifth of April.*
u primu di maggiu   *The first of May*

(c) *A couple* or *a pair* is **un paru**; *the plural is* **para**

    un paru di scarpi *a pair of shoes.*

(d) The **-ina** suffix indicates *about, some*, as in **una decina**, **una vintina**, **una trentina**, etc. but **una duzzina** is *a dozen.*

una cinquantina di libbri *some fifty books*
una duzzina di libbri   *a dozen books*

(e) *Once, twice*, etc. are **una vota, dui voti**, etc

Vinni â casa **tri voti**   *He came to the house three times*

(f) *Several times* is **paricchi voti**

U visti **paricchi voti**   *I saw it several times.*

71

ESERCIZI: Translate the following into Sicilian:

1. Some thirty houses. 2. Two pairs of shoes. 3. Pippinuzza has two dozen books. 4. It is 4:30. 5. The sixth of May. 6. Two thousand one hundred

LEZZIONI SESTA   NTÔ RISTORANTI

Ninu: Stamatina dumannai ô gerenti di l'albergu pir un ristoranti chi specializza in pitanzi siciliani e mi detti u nomi di una osteria cca vicinu.

Maria: Comu si chiama?

Ninu: Osteria da Turiddu. E dissi chi ci putemu iri a pedi in un attimu.

Maria: Tutti dui havemu fami, perciò, avanti! Iamuninni!
Doppu cincu minuti arrivanu a l'Osteria da Turiddu.

Ninu: Una tavula pi' dui, pir favuri. *Quannu sunu assittati, u camareri ci duna a lista.*Camareri, stasira vulemu mangiari pitanzi siciliani. Chi ni raccumanna?

Camareri: Pir accuminciari, vi raccumannu a pitanza speciali di Palermu, pasta chî sardi. Si pripara cu sardi frischi e finocchiu sarvaggiu. E poi, pi' secunnariu, pisci spata affumicatu, cu cuntorni di patati ô furnu e funci fritti.

Ninu: Benissimu. E du beddu panuzzu sicilianu.

Camareri: Ma certu. E na insalata mista. E comu vinu, forsi una buttigghia di Donnafugata, un vinu palermitanu biancu, friscu, friscu.

Quannu hannu finitu a cena, paganu u contu, pani e cupertu e na mancia pû camareri, e, cuntenti, tornanu a l'albergu.

73

LESSON SIX   AT THE RESTAURANT

Ninu: This morning I asked the hotel manager for a restaurant that specializes in Sicilian foods and he gave me the nameof a nearby restaurant.

Maria: What is it called?

Ninu: Turiddu's Tavern. He said that we can get there in no time.

Maria: We're both hungry, so, forward march! Let's go!
They get to Turiddu's Tavern in five minutes.

Ninu: A table for two, please *When they are seated, the waiter gives them a menu.*Waiter, tonight we want to eat some Sicilian food. What do you recommend?

Camareri: To begin with, I recommend Palermo's specialty, pasta with sardines. It is prepared with fresh sardines and wild fennel. Then as a second dish, smoked swordfish, with a side dish of roasted potatoes and fried mushrooms.

Ninu: Fine. And some of that wonderful Sicilian bread.

Camareri: Of course. And a mixed salad. And as for wine, perhaps a bottle of Donnafugata, a very fresh Palermitan white wine. *When they have finished, they pay the bill and cover and give the waiter a tip; then, quite content, they return to the hotel.*

VOCABULARY

accuminciari	to begin
affumicatu	smoked
assittati	seated
attimu	instant
avanti	forward (march)
beddu	wonderful
biancu	white
buttigghia	bottle
camareri	waiter
cca	here
cena	dinner
chî	with (the)
chiama, si	it is called
ci	them
comu	how, what, as to
contu	bill
cu	with
cuntenti	content, happy
cuntorni	side dish
da Turiddu	Turiddu's
detti	he gave
dissi	he said
du	that
dumannai	I asked
duna	gives
finitu	finished
finocchiu	fennel
forsi	perhaps
frischi	fresh
friscu, friscu	quite fresh

fritti	fried
funci	mushrooms
gerenti	manager
iamuninni	let's go
insalata	salad
lista	menu
mancia	tip
mangiari	to eat
mi	me
minuti	minutes
mista	mixed
na	a, an
ni	(to) us
nomi	name
osteria	tavern
paganu	they pay
palermitanu	Palermitan
pani e cupertu	cover
panuzzu	lovely bread
pasta	pasta
patati ô furnu	roasted potatoes
perciò	therefore
pir favuri	please
pisci spata	sword fish
pitanzi	foods
poi	then
pripara (si)	it is prepared
pû	for the
raccumanna	recommend
sardi	(fresh) sardines
sarvaggiu	wild
secunnariu	second (dish)
speciali	special

specializza	specializes
stamatina	this morning
stasira	tonight
tavula	table
tornanu	they return
vi	(to) you
vinu	wine
vicinu	near
vulemu	we want

LOCUZIONI

EXPRESSIONS

pitanzi siciliani	Sicilian dishes
cca vicinu	nearby
in un attimu	in an instant
avanti	foward (march)
iamuninni	let us go
Osteria da Turiddu	Turiddu's Tavern
una tavula pi' dui	a table for two
pir favuri	please
chi ni raccumanna?	what do you recommend?
pir accuminzari	to begin with
pasta chî sardi	pasta with sardines
finocchiu sarvaggiu	wild fennel
pi' secunnariu	second dish
pisci spata affumicatu	smoked swordfish
patati ô furnu	baked potatoes
una buttigghia di Donnafugata	a bottle of Donnafugata wine
u beddu panuzzu sicilianu	the wonderful Sicilian bread
na insalata mista	a mixed salad
paganu u contu	they pay the bill
pani e cupertu	cover
na mancia pû camareri	a tip for the waiter

ESERCIZI   EXERCISES

1. Copy the text, read it aloud and translate it.

2. Make up sentences with the following phrases and repeat them
three times:
paganu u contu; pitanzi siciliani; cca vicinu; in un attimu

3. Translate into Sicilian:
Let's go!; we want to eat some Sicilian food; I recommend
Palermo's special food; the waiter gives them a menu

4. Translate into English:
u beddu panuzzu sicilianu; na mancia pû camareri ; chi ni
raccumanna?; una tavula pi' dui

5. Memorize:
pasta chî sardi; in un attimu; comu si chiama? iamuninni

GRAMMAR

VI. Pronouns

Personal Pronouns

There are two types of personal pronouns:
disjunctive and **conjunctive**

A.Disjunctive Pronouns

These pronouns do not receive the action of the verb;
as it were, they are <u>dis</u>-joined from it.

There are two types of disjunctives:

1.<u>Subject Pronouns</u>, used as the subject of a verb and
2.<u>Object Pronouns</u>, used only after prepositions.

1. Subject Pronouns

These are used as the subject of a verb.

Singular	Plural
<u>iu</u> **parru**, *I speak*	<u>nuautri</u> [nui] **parramu**, *we speak*
<u>tu</u> **parri**, *you speak*	<u>vuautri</u> [vui] **parrati**, *you speak*
<u>iddu</u>, **parra**, *he (it) speaks*	<u>iddi</u>, *m*, **parranu**, *they speak*
<u>idda</u>, **parra**, *she (it) speaks*	<u>iddi</u>, *f*, **parranu**, *they speak*

Nui and vui are used only in some parts of Sicily. The familiar **tu**
form is used in addressing children, relatives, close friends, servants
and persons of a lower social rank.

The subject pronouns are generally omitted, but are always used for clearness.

Parramu chiaru.	*We speak clearly.*
Iu u fazzu, non iddu.	*I do it, not he.*

2. Object Pronouns

These are used as the object of a preposition. **pir iddu** , *for him,* **a idda** , *to her*

m*i***a**, me	**nu***au***tri**, us
t*i***a**, you	**v***ua***tri**, you
iddu , he, it	**iddi** , they, *m.*
idda , she, it	**iddi** , they, *f.*

Filippu veni cu **m***i***a**.	*Philip comes with me.*
U fa pir **nu***au***tri**.	*He does it for us.*
Tu dugnu a **t***i***a**.	*I give it to you.*

B. Conjunctive Pronouns

These forms are so called because they stand next to, and precede the verb (**con-** ,*with*); as it were, they are joined-with the verb (**-junct-**), which they sometimes follow, but often precede. They serve as the direct object of a verb (d.o.), and as indirect object without a preposition (i.o.); they are as follows:

Singular		Plural	
(d.o.) (i.o.)		(d.o.) (i.o.)	
mi, *me, to me*		**ni**, *us, to us*	
ti, *you, to you*		**vi**, *you, to you*	
u, *him,* **ci**, *to him*		**i**, *them,* **ci**, *to them* (m)	
a, *her,* **ci**, *to her*		**i**, *them,* **ci**, *to them* (f)	

80

Singular

(d.o.) **Mi** tal*i*a.	*He looks at me.*
(i.o.) Maria **mi** duna u libbru.	*Mary gives me the book.*
(d.o.) **Ti** canusci.	*He knows you.*
(i.o.) Filippu **ti** duna u libbru.	*Philip gives you the book.*
(d.o.) **U**(**a**) vidu ddocu.	*I see him (her) there.*
(i.o.) **Ci** parru chiaru.	*I speak to him (her) clearly.*

Plural

(d.o.) Me matri **ni** voli beni.	*My mother loves us.*
(i.o.) Iddu **ni** parra cu sincerità.	*He speaks to us sincerely.*
(d.o.) Carlu **vi** talia.	*Charles looks at you.*
(i.o.) Anna **vi** coci a pasta.	*Anna cooks pasta for you.*
(d.o.) **I** amu comu me figghi.	*I love them as my sons.*
(i.o.) **Ci** vuliti dari i puma?	*Will you give them the apples?*

1. Reflexive pronouns are conjunctive:

mi, *myself*   **ni**, *ourselves*
ti, *yourself*   **vi**, *yourselves*
si, *himself, herself*   **si**, *themselves* (m.,f.)

Mi vestu. *I dress myself.*   **Ni** vistimu. *We dress ourselves.*
Ti vesti. *You dress yourself*   **Vi** vistiti. *You dress yourselves.*
Si vesti. *He, she dresses*   **Si** vestinu. *They dress*
         himself, herself   *themselves*

2. Another conjunctive pronoun is **ni**, *of it, of them, any, some; any, some of them.* It serves the same purpose as the French **en** and the Italian **ne**.

Nun **ni** avemu.   *We don't have any.*
Ni vuliti?   *Do you want any?*

3. Conjunctive pronouns immediately precede the verb:

    Mi viditi. *You see me.*
  Unn **u** capisciu. *I don't understand him.*

<u>But</u> when the verb is (a) <u>an infinitive(inf)</u>, (b) <u>a positive imperative</u>
<u>(pos.imp)</u>,or (c)<u> a present participle(pres. part.)</u>, <u>the pronoun</u>
<u>follows the verb and is written as one word with it.</u>

   (inf) (a) pi v*i*dir**lu**, *to see him*
       di avir**lu** vistu, *to have seen him*
  (pos.imp) (b) vid*i*ti**li**, *see them*
       damm**ilu**, *give it to me*
 (pres. part) (c) av**ennuci** vistu, *having seen us*
       vid**ennuci**, *seeing us*

4. The conjunctive pronouns **mi,ti, ci, ni, vi** precede **lu, la** and
 li and unite with them.

  Milu dici. *He tells it to me.*
  Tila cunta (sta storia). *He tells it to you(this tale).*
  Cili duna. *He gives them to them.*
  Nili vinni. *He sells them to us.*
  Vili mannu. *I send them to you.*

ESERCIZI: Translate the following into Sicilian:

1. We dress ourselves. 2. He does it for me. 3. Give it to me.
4. I don't want it. 5. He gives them to you. 6. Do you want any?
7. Carl gives me the book. 8. She dresses herself. 9. They speak.

LEZZIONI SETTIMA GIRARI I PUTII

Maria: Ninu, chi ti pari - oggi putemu girari i putii?

Ninu: Pirchì no? Unna voi iri prima?

Maria: In un negozziu di vistuariu.

Ninu: Allura, iamu.

Ntô negozziu.

Maria, *â commissa*: Vogghiu vidiri una vistina eleganti in blu.

A Commissa: Eccu, una bellissima.

Maria: A pozzu pruvari?

A Commissa: Ma certu.

Maria, *doppu avirla pruvatu*: Mi sta beni. Ninu, ti piaci?

Ninu: Si, mì piaci assai.

Maria:Quantu custa?

A Commissa: Ottantacincu mila liri.

Maria: È troppu cara...nun ti pari, Ninu?

Ninu: Si, ma è una bella vistina e pagamu u prezzu.*Paganu u* *cascieri e nescinu dô negozziu.* E ora, unna iemu, Maria'?

Maria: Vulissi iri â farmacia chi è cca vicinu. *Ntâ farmacia,ô farmacista.* Haiu bisognu di aspirina, una butigghia di acqua dentifricia pir sciacquari a vucca, e un tubettu di pasta dentifricia.

Farmacista: Nenti di chiù?

Ninu: Mi bisogna un tubettu di crema di varva.

Farmacista *doppu cincu minuti:* Eccu. *Ninu paga e nescinu dâ farmacia.*

Ninu: E ora unna voi iri, Maria?

Maria: Bisognu truvari una sala di biddizza.

Ninu: Ma tu si accussì bedda chi unn hai bisogna di sala di biddizza.

Maria E tu, Ninu, sempri chi scherzi.

Ninu: Eccu a sala di biddizza, bedda. *Trasinu e Maria parra cû gerenti.*

Maria: Quannu pozzu viniri pir un' ondulazioni permanenti?

U Gerenti: Po viniri dumani ê novi?

Maria: Sì, milli grazii.

LESSON SEVEN   SHOPPING AROUND

Maria: Ninu, what do you think - can we go shopping today?

Ninu: Why not? Where do you want to go first?

Maria: To a dress shop.

Ninu: Well, then, let's go. *At the shop.*

Maria, *to the saleslady:* I'd like to see a stylish blue dress.

A Commissa: Here you are. A beauty.

Maria: May I try it on?

A Commissa: Of course.

Maria, *after having tried it on:* It looks good on me. Do you like it, Ninu?

Ninu: Yes, very much.

Maria: How much does it cost?

A Commissa: 85,000 liras.

Maria: That's too expensive...don't you think so, Ninu?

Ninu: Yes, but it's a beautiful dress and we'll pay the price.
They pay the cashier and leave the store. Where do we go now, Maria?

Maria: I'd like to go to the drug store which is nearby *At the drugstore, to the farmacist.* I meed aspirins, a bottle of mouthwash to rinse my mouth and a tube of toothpaste.

Farmacista: Nothing else?

Ninu: I need a tube of shaving cream.

Farmacista *after five minute:* There you are. *Ninu pays and they leave the pharmacy.*

Ninu: Where do you want to go now, Maria?

Maria: I must find a beauty parlor.

Ninu: But you're so beautiful that you don't need a beauty parlor.

Maria: Ninu, you're always joking.

Ninu: Here's the beauty parlor, beautiful. *They enter and Maria speaks with the manager.*

Maria: When can I come for a permanent?

U Gerenti: Can you come tomorrow at nine?

Maria: Yes, many thanks.

VOCABULARY

acqua dentifricia	mouthwash
aspirina	aspirin
assai	a lot
bedda	beautiful
bellissima	very beautiful
beni	well
blu	blue
butigghia	bottle
cara	dear, expensive
cascieri	cashier
commissa	saleslady
crema di varva	shaving cream
cû	with the
custa	it costs
eleganti	stylish
ê novi	at nine o'clock
farmacìa	drug store
farmacista	pharmacist
gerenti	manager
girari	tour
negozziu	shop
nescinu	they leave
ondulazioni permanenti	a permanent
ottantacincu	eighty-five
pagamu	we ('ll) pay
pari	seem to you
parra	he, she speaks
pasta dentifricia	tooth paste
piaci	you like
pirchì	why

pozzu	I can
prezzu	price
prima	first
pruvatu	tried
pruvari	to try
putii	shops
quantu	how much
sala di biddizza	beauty parlor
scherzi	you joke
sciacquari	rinse
sempri	always
sta	is, fits, looks
trasinu	they enter
troppu	too much
truvari	to find
tubettu	tube
unna	where
vidiri	to see
viniri	to come
vistina	dress
vistuariu	clothing
voi	you want
vucca	mouth
vulissi	I would want

LOCUZIONI

EXPRESSIONS

chi ti pari?	what do you think?
girari i putii	to go shopping
un negozziu di vistuariu	a dress shop
una vistina eleganti	a stylish dress
a pozzu pruvari?	may I try it on?
mi sta beni	it looks good on me

ti piaci?	do you like it?
mi piaci assai	I like it very much
quantu custa?	how much does it cost?
è troppu cara	it's too expensive
nun ti pari?	don't you think so?
pagamu u prezzu	we'll pay the price
nescinu dô negozziu	they leave the shop
è cca vicinu	it's nearby
una butigghia di acqua dentifricia	a bottle of mouthwash
pir sciacquari a vucca	to rinse the mouth
un tubettu di pasta dentifricia	a tube of toothpaste
nenti di chiù?	nothing else?
crema di varva	shaving cream
una sala di biddizza	a beauty parlor
sempri chi scherzi	you're always joking
parra cû gerenti	she speaks with the manager
un' ondulazioni permanenti	a permanent

ESERCIZI

EXERCISES

1. Copy the text, read it aloud and translate it.

2. Make up sentences with the following phrases and repeat them three times:
nenti di chiù?; un tubettu di pasta dentifricia; quantu custa?; girari i putii

3. Translate into Sicilian:
Ninu, you're always joking; when can I come for a permanent?; It looks good on me; they leave the shop.

4. Translate into English:
una vistina eleganti; a pozzu pruvari?; una sala di biddizza; una butigghia di acqua dentifricia;

5. Memorize:
chi ti pari? girari i putii; sempri chi scherzi; una sala di biddizza; quantu custa?

GRAMMAR

VII. Adjectives and Pronouns

A.Demonstrative Adjectives and Pronouns
agree in number and gender with the noun they modify or represent.

<u>**Adjectives**</u>   <u>**Pronouns**</u>

(a) <u>Near the speaker:</u> **this**

stu (m), **sta**(f), **sti**(pl)   **chistu**(m), **chista**(f), **chisti**(pl)

stu libbru, *this book*   **chistu**, *this one*
sta fimmina,*this woman*   **chista**, *this one*
sti puma, *these apples*   **chisti**, *these*

(b) <u>Near the person addressed:</u> **that**

su (m), **sa**(f), **si**(pl)   **chissu** (m), **chissa** (f), **chissi** (pl)

su libbru, *that book*   **chissu**, *that one*
sa fimmina,*that woman*   **chissa**, *that one*
si puma, *those apples*   **chissi**, *those*

(c) <u>Away from the speaker or the person addressed:</u> **that**

du (m), **da**(f), **di**(pl)   **chiddu** (m), **chidda**(f),**chiddi** (pl)

du libbru, *that book* (*over there*)   **chiddu**, *that one*
da fimmina,*that woman*   **chidda**, *that one*
di puma, *those apples*   **chiddi**, *those*

B. Interrogatives, Possessives

1. The interrogative *who, whom*, is **cu.**

Cu veni stasira?	*Who is coming tonight?*
A **cu** vidu?	*Whom do I see?*

2. *What* ? used as a pronoun is **chi,** used as an adjective is **chi** or **quali. ** *Which*? is **quali** . *How much*? *How many* is **quantu.** All are invariable.

Chi vidi?	*What do you see?*
Chi *or* **quali** libbri accattasti?	*What books did you buy?*
Quantu soldi guadagnasti?	*How much money did you earn?*
Quantu voti ti l'haiu dittu?	*How many times have I told you*

C. Relative Pronouns

The principal relative pronouns are **chi, cui, u (a, i) quali**: they apply to both persons and things, and mean *who, whom, which* ,or *that*. **Chi** and **cui** are invariable: in general **chi** is used only as subject and direct object, **cui** only after prepositions or as indirect object. **Cu**, *who*, applies to persons.

A lingua **chi** si parra cca.	*The language (that is) spoken here*.
A figghia **chi** studia.	*The daughter who is studying*
I fimmini a **cui** parru.	*The women to whom I speak*.

1. *What*, meaning *that which*, is **zaccu** (pronounced TSAK ku*)*;it is invariable.

   Unu sacciu **zaccu** dici.　　*I don't know what he is saying*.

93

D. Possessive Adjectives and Pronouns

	Singular M.F.		Plural M.F.	
	Adj.	Pron.	Adj.	Pron.
my,mine:	me	u (a) mè	me	i mè
your,yours:	to	u (a) tò	to	i tò
his,her(s):	so	u (a) sò	so	i sò
our,ours:	nostru	u (a) nostra	nostri	i nostri
your,yours:	vostru	u (a)vostra	vostri	i vostri
their,theirs:	so	u (a) sò	so	i sò

Me, to, so are invariable (i.e. do not agree with the noun in number and gender), but **nostru** and **vostru** do agree with the noun in number and gender.

Adj.	Pron.
me libbru, *my book.*	**u sò**, *his (book).*
so figghia, *his daughter*	**a sò**, *his (daughter)*
so figghi, *his, their daughters*	**i sò**, *theirs (daughters)*
nostra matri, *our mother*	**i sò**, *theirs (mothers)*

ESERCIZI: Translate the following into Sicilian:
1.Our daughter is beautiful. 2.This book is his. 3.The man to whom I speak. 4. Who is speaking? 5. That woman (over there) is beautiful. 6.Our mother and theirs.7.How much money does it cost? 8.Whom do you see? 9. This one is good.

LEZZIONI OTTAVA

IN CAMINU

Ninu: Unn è bedda sta machina chi ni fici prenutari a Hertz nî Stati Uniti? Haiu a patenti di guida internazionali e ora putemu accuminciari u nostru viaggiu a San Fratello, unna fummu invitati a passari du' iorna câ famigghia di Gianni e Anna Orlando.

Maria: Quantu ni custa u nuliggiu da machina?

Ninu: È cara; tri centu cinquanta dollari â simana. A benzina puru è cara— un dollaru e vinti cincu ô litru. E poi duvemu pagari una tassa di quasi cincu dollari pir viaggiari ntâ autostrata di Palermo a Messina. Insumma, è un pocu caru, ma vali a pena, unn ti pari?

Maria: Ma certu.Dunca, avanti, in caminu.
Doppu un ura di viaggiu lungu a costa, arrivanu a Cefalù.

Ninu: Eccu Cefalù, Maria, un beddu paiseddu fattu apposta pî turisti cu una spiaggia pulita e un domu cu musaici bizantini chi fannu rammintari a cattedrali di Monreale.

Maria: Pirchì unn facemu un picculu giru a pedi prima di pranzari in unu di sti ristoranti?

Ninu: Una bona idea. E doppu u pranzu putemu cuntinuari in caminu a San Fratello.

LESSON EIGHT

ON THE ROAD

Ninu: This is a nice car that Hertz reserved for us back in the States. I have an international driver's license and so now we can begin our trip to San Fratello, where we were invited to spend a couple of days with Gianni and Anna Orlando's family.

Maria: How much does the car rental cost?

Ninu: It's expensive; three hundred and fifty dollars a week. Gas is expensive, too— a dollar and a quarter a liter. Then we have to pay a five dollar toll on the highway from Palermo to Messina. In short, it's a bit expensive, but it's worth while, don't you think?

Maria: I certainly do...Well, then, onward, let's hit the road. *They arrive at Cefalù after an hour's trip along the coast.*

Ninu: Here's Cefalù, Maria, a nice little town made to order for tourists, with a clean beach and a cathedral with beautiful byzantine mosaics that remind one of the cathedral at Monreale.

Maria: Why don't we do a short tour on foot before having lunch at one of these restaurants?

Ninu: A good idea. And after lunch we can continue on our way to San Fratello.

VOCABULARY

accuminciari	to begin
apposta	especially
arrivanu	they arrive
autostrata	road, highway
benzina	gasoline
bizantini	Byzantine
caminu (in)	on the road
cara	expensive
cattedrali	cathedral
costa	coast
cuntinuari	continue
domu	dome, cathedral
doppu	after
duvemu	we must
famigghia	family
fattu	made
fummu	we were
guida	driver's
haiu	I have
idea	idea
insumma	in short, so then
internazionali	international
invitati	invited
lungu	along
machina	auto, car
musaici	mosaics
nuliggiu	rent
ntâ	on the
pagari	pay
paiseddu	small town
passari	to spend

97

patenti	license
pena	while (pity)
picculu	small, short
pocu	a bit, somewhat
poi	then
pranzari	lunch(ing)
pranzu	lunch
prenutari	to reserve
prima	before
pulita	clean
putemu	we can
quasi	almost
rammintari	remember, recall
simana	week
spiaggia	beach
tassa	tax, toll
turisti	tourists
vali	is worth
viaggiari	to travel
viaggiu	trip

LOCUZIONI

EXPRESSIONS

a patenti di guida internazionali	international driver's license
fummu invitati	we were invited
quantu ni custa?	how much does it cost?
u nuliggiu da machina	the car rental
è un pocu caru	it's somewhat expensive
vali a pena	it's worth while
unn ti pari?	don't you think so?
dunca	well, then
doppu un ura di viaggiu	after travelling an hour
lungu a costa	along the coast

eccu Cefalù	here's Cefalù
un beddu paiseddu	a nice little town
fattu apposta pî turisti	made to order for tourists
una spiaggia pulita	a clean beach
musaici bizantini	byzantine mosaics
fannu rammintari	remind one
prima di pranzari	before having lunch
in unu di sti ristoranti	in one of these restaurants
una bona idea	a good idea

ESERCIZI   EXERCISES

1. Copy the text, read it aloud and translate it.

2. Make up sentences with the following phrases and repeat them
three times:
una bona idea; fannu rammintari;un beddu paiseddu; lungu a costa.

3. Translate into Sicilian:
made to order for tourists; a nice little town; we have to pay a five
dollar toll; after travelling an hour.

4. Translate into English:
tri centu cinquanta dollari â simana; haiu a patenti di guida
internazionali; a benzina puru è cara; ma vali a pena, unn ti pari?

5. Memorize:
unn ti pari? lungu a costa; ; una sala di biddizza; una bona idea;
quantu ni custa?

99

VIII.Indefinite Adjectives & Pronouns; Conjunctions and Prepositions

A.Indefinite Adjectives & Pronouns

(a) _Si_ , as an indefinite pronoun, used as the subject of a verb, is translated as *one*, *people*, *we*, *you*, or *they*,

Si mangia beni in Sicilia.	*One eats well in Sicily.*
Si fa accussì.	*You do it this way.*

(b) _Any_

— when it really adds nothing to the sense, is omitted:

Unn havi libbri.	*He doesn't have (any) books.*
Vuliti vinu?	*Do you want any wine?*

— meaning *any of it*, *any of them* is **ni**.

Unn **ni** haiu.	*I haven't any.*
Unn **ni** havi chiù.	*He doesn't have any anymore.*
Ni aviti?	*Do you have any?*

(c) *One...another (both)* is *l'unu...l' autru*

Voi sasizza or du'ova?	*Do you want sausages or two eggs?*
L'unu e l'autru .	*Both (one and the other).*

100

(d)The following are some common indefinite pronouns and adjectives (a reference list):

anybody, **qualcunu** , pron.
anything, **qualchicosa** , pron.
both, **tutti dui**, **l'unu e l'autru**
each,every, **ogni** ,adj., **ognunu** , pron.
either, **l'unu o l' autru**, pron.or adj.
everybody, **ognunu,** pron.
everything, **tuttu**, pron.
few, a few, **pochi,** pron.or adj.
little, **pocu** , pron.or adj.

less, **menu** , pron.or adj.
many, several, **paricchi**
more, **chiù** , pron.or adj.
neither, **nè l'unu nè**
l'autru , pron.or adj.
nobody, **nessunu,nuddu**
nothing, **nenti, nulla**
somebody, **qualcunu**
something, **qualchicosa**

B. Conjunctions and Prepositions   (a reference list)

<u>Conjunctions</u>

Some common conjunctions are:

after, **doppu chi**
although, **benchì**
and, **e**
as, **comu**
as(since), **siccomu**
because, **pirchì**
before, **prima chi**
but, **ma**
if, **si**
neither...nor, **nè...nè**
nor, **nè**
or, **o**
rather, **anzi**

since (causal), **siccomu** , **giacchì**
so, **dunca**
so that , **di modu chi**
than,that, **chi**
that, (in order that), **pirchì**
then, **dunca**
therefore, **dunca, però** , **perciò**
unless, **a menu chi**
when, **quannu**
whence, **di unni**
where, **unni**
whether, **sì**
while, **mentri**

101

Prepositions

Some common prepositions are:

about (approximately), **circa**	*in*, **in**
about (around), **intornu a**	*in front of*, **davanti a**
above, **supra**	*inside of*, **dintra di**
according to, **secunnu**	*instead of*, **inveci di**
after, **doppu**	*in the midst of*, **nu menzu di**
against, **contra**	*into*, **in, dintra**
along, **accantu**	*near*, **vicinu a**
among, **fra**	*of*, **di**
as far as, **sinu a**	*on, over*, **su , supra**
as to, **quantu a**	*opposite*, **dirrimpettu**
before (time), **prima di**	*out of,outside of*, **fora di**
behind, **darreri**	*round and round*, **intornu (a)**
below, under, **sutta**	*toward*, **versu**
between,within, **fra**	*through*, **pir,** or a
by means of, **pir menzu di**	*up to*, **sinu**
during, **duranti**	*with*, **cu**
except, **eccettu , tranni**	*without*, **senza**
from, **da**	

Note the following uses:

1. *To* is omitted before an infinitive following an auxiliary verb:

Devi capiri.	*He ought <u>to</u> understand.*
Putemu viniri.	*We'll be able <u>to</u> come.*
Nun sapi zaccu fari.	*He doesn't know what <u>to</u> do.*

2. Only an infinitive may be used as the object of a preposition and not the present participle as in English.

102

Cuntò a munita prima di pagari.	*He counted his money before* <u>*paying*</u>.
Si fici capiri senza parrari.	*He made himself understood without* <u>*speaking*</u>.

3. **Da** has varied meanings:

(a) <u>Characteristic of</u>·

A sala **da** pranzu.	*The dining room.*

(b) <u>from:</u>

Arrivò oggi **da** Parigi.	*He arrived from Paris today.*

(c) <u>by:</u>

Fu fattu **da** Ninu.	*It was done by Nino.*

(d) **Da** corresponds to English *on, at,* or *to* before the word *side,*and *as far as one is concerned:*

Da chista parti.	*On this side.*
Da so parti, Gianni...	*As far as he' s concerned, John...*

(e) <u>as a:</u>

Prumettu **da** omu d'onuri.	*I promise as a man of honor.*

(f) *to,* indicating duty or necessity:

Havi qualchicosa **da** fari.	*He has something to do.*

103

ESERCIZI: Translate the following into Sicilian:
1.Does he have any? 2.He doesn't know what to do. 3.He arrived from Rome today. 4. It was done by Maria. 5.Our mother and theirs.6.How much money does it cost? 7.Whom do you see? 8. This one is good. 9. He has nothing to do.

LEZZIONI NONA   OSPITI A SAN FRATELLO

Maria: Ora chi avemu lassatu Sant'Agata di Militello accuminciamu l'acchianata di dumila ducentu pedi pir un caminu chi gira e gira finu a San Fratello.

Ninu: St'acchianata quasi chi fa girari a testa.

Maria: È un paiseddu pitturiscu postu su una pendenza panoramica dî Monti Nebrodi... Talia, Ninu, talia, avemu arrivatu, e di cca si po vidiri u Mari Tirrenu.

Ninu: Sì, ora capisciu pirchì i Normanni, quannu hannu scunfiggitu i Saraceni ntô undicesimu seculu e l'hannucacciatu fora dâ Sicilia, hannu fattu di San Fratello na furtizza chi domina u Tirrenu.

Maria: Ninu, mi pari chi avemu arrivatu; chista devi essiri acasa di Gianni e Anna. *Pochi momenti doppu, sunu ricivuti da Gianni e Anna.*

Ninu: *Porgi un mazzu di sciuri a Anna.* Pâ signura dâ casa.

Anna: Chi gentilizza; milli grazii.

Gianni: Datemi i valliggetti e seguitimi â cammara dî ospiti.
Quannu siti arrizzitati viniti ntô salottu pir un aperitivu.
Doppu l'aperitivu passanu â sala da pranzu.
Oggi mangiamu u pisci stoccu, una pitanza tipica di sti parti.

Maria: Chi sapuri incantevuli. Mi vuliti dari a ricetta?

Anna: Vulunteri. E dumani facemu un giru di sta città storica.

LESSON NINE   GUESTS IN SAN FRATELLO

Maria: Now that we have left Sant'Agata di Militello,we begin the climb of 2,200 feet on a road that turns and turns until it reaches San Fratello.

Ninu: This climb almost makes one's head spin.

Maria: It's a picturesque town located on a panoramic slopeof the Nebrodi Mountain... Look, Ninu, look, we've arrivedand from here one can see the Tyrrhenian Sea.

Ninu: Now I understand why the Normans made San Fratellointo a fortress that dominates the Tyrrhenian, when they routed the Saracens out of Sicily in the 11th century.

Maria: Ninu, I think we've arrived; this must be Gianni's and Anna's house. *A few moments later, they are welcomed by Gianni and Anna.*

Ninu: *He hands Anna a bouquet of flowers* For the lady of the house.

Anna: How kind of you; many thanks.

Gianni: Let me have your valises and follow me to the guest room. When you have settled in, come to the living room for an aperitif. *After which, they go to the dining room.*Today, we're going to eat stockfish, a dish typical of theseparts.

Maria: What an enchanting flavor. May I have the recipe.

Anna: Willingly. Tomorrow we'll tour this historic city.

VOCABULARY

acchianata	climb
aperitivu	aperitif
arrizzitati	settled
cacciatu	chased
cammara dî ospiti	guest room
capisciu	I understand
casa	house
città	city
dari	to give
datemi	give me
domina	dominates
fa	makes
facemu	we do
finu	up to
fora	out
furtizza	fortress
gentilizza	gentility
gira	turns
incantevuli	enchanting
lassatu	departed from
mangiamu	we shall eat
Mari Tirrenu	Tyrrhenian Sea
mazzu	bouquet
momenti	moments
oggi	today
ospiti	guests
panoramica	panoramic
parti	parts
passanu	pass
pendenza	slope
pisci stoccu	stockfish

107

pitanza	dish
pitturiscu	picturesque
porgi	hands
postu	place
quasi	almost
ricetta	recipe
ricivuti	received
sala da pranzu	dining room
salottu	living room
sapuri	taste
Saraceni	Saracens
sciuri	flowers
scunfiggitu	defeated
seculu	century
seguitimi	follow me
signura	lady
storica	historic
testa	head
típica	typical
valliggetti	valises
viniti	come
vuliti	you wish
vulunteri	willingly

LOCUZIONI

EXPRESSIONS

ora chi avemu lassatu	now that we have left
accuminciamu l'acchianata	we begin the climb
un caminu chi gira e gira	a road that turns and turns
finu a	up to
quasi chi fa girari a testa	it almost makes one's head swim
un paiseddu pitturiscu	a picturesque little town

una pendenza panoramica	a panoramic slope
si po vidiri	one can see
hannu scunfiggitu	they defeated
hannu cacciatu fora	they threw out
chista devi essiri	this must be
pochi momenti doppu	a few moments later
porgi un mazzu di sciuri	hands a bouquet
pâ signura dâ casa	for the lady of the house
chi gentilizza	how kind of you
â cammara dî ospiti	to the guest room
quannu siti arrizzitati	when you're settled in
a sala da pranzu	the dining room
una pitanza tipica di sti parti	a dish typical of these parts
chi sapuri incantevuli	what a delightful taste
vulunteri	willingly

ESERCIZI

EXERCISES

1. Copy the text, read it aloud and translate it.

2. Make up sentences with the following phrases and repeat them
three times:
fa girari a testa; chi sapuri incantevuli; hannu cacciatu fora; un
caminu chi gira e gira.

3. Translate into Sicilian:
what a delightful taste; a picturesque little town ; a road that turns
and turns; a panoramic slope; a dish typical of these parts

4. Translate into English:
vulunteri; accuminciamu l'acchianata; hannu cacciatu fora; quasi chi
fa girari a testa; porgi un mazzu di sciuri.

5. Memorize:
un paiseddu pitturiscu; chi sapuri incantevuli; pâ signura dâ casa;
quannu siti arrizzitati; chi gentilizza

IX. Adverbs

Adverbs do not agree with nouns, adjectives, or verbs.
They are invariable.

There are two types of adverbs: <u>conjunctive</u> and <u>disjunctive</u>

<u>Conjunctive</u>, so called because they stand next to, and precede the
verb (**con** -*with*).

1. **ci** (there)

(a) indicating place:

Va a Roma? No, nun **ci** va.　　*Is he going to Rome? No, he's not*
　　　　　　　　　　　　　　　　going.

(b) used emphatically at the beginning of a phrase:

　　　　C'era una vota.　　*Once upon a time.*

2. **ni** (of it, etc) An unemphatic adverbial pronoun referring to a
prepositional phrase introduced by **di**.

Ha parratu <u>di so patri</u>?　　*Has he spoken of his father?*
Sì, **ni** havi parratu.　　　　*Yes, he has spoken of him.*

111

<u>Disjunctive</u>, so called because they do not receive the action of the verb; as it were, they are <u>dis</u>-joined from it. There are four groups of disjunctives: <u>of place; of time; of quantity; and of manners.</u>

1. Adverbs of Place

Cca, here, near the speaker. *Ddocu,* there, near the person addressed. *Dda,* over there, away from both. *Vicinu,* nearby, close. *Luntanu,* distant, far.

Unna è? È **cca**.	*Where is it? It's here.*
Chi fai **ddocu?**	*What are you doing there?*
U vidu **dda**.	*I see him over there.*
A so casa è **vicinu**.	*His house is nearby.*
A cità è **luntanu**.	*The city is far away.*

2. Adverbs of Time

non ...mai, *never*	**stasira** , *this evening*
ora, *now*	**stanotti** , *last night*
ora ora, *right away*	**avantaieri** , *day before yesterday*
spissu , *often*	**aieri**, *yesterday*
sempri , *always*	**dumani** , *tomorrow*
prestu , *soon*	**aierisira** , *last night*
oggi , *today*	**doppu dumani** , *day after*
stamatina , *this morning*	*tomorrow*
fa, *ago*	

Non ti ha **mai** parratu.	*He has never spoken to you.*
U fazzu **ora ora**.	*I'll do it right away.*
Tri anni **fa**.	*Three years ago.*
Arrivò **aierisira**.	*He arrived last night.*

112

Ci vaiu **doppu dumani.**   *I'll go the day after tomorrow.*
Iddu è **sempri** mansu.   *He is always well-behaved.*

3. Adverbs of Quantity

assai , *a lot, much, enough*   **tantu**, *much, so much*
troppu , *too much, too*   **pocu** , *little, small, few*
        tuttu, *all, whole, entire*

Ti voli ben' **assai** .   *He is very fond of you.*
Sugnu **troppu** stancu.   *I am too tired.*

4. Adverbs of Manner

(a) Adverbs of manner are formed by adding the suffix **-menti** to
the feminine form of the adjective.

chiaru , *clear*   **chiaramenti** , *clearly*
francu , *frank*   **francamenti** , *frankly*

However, Sicilians prefer using the adjective as an adverb.

Unn pozzu v*i*diri troppu **bonu.**   *I can't see too well.*
Iddu parra **chiaru** .   *He speaks clearly.*

(b) So meaning *it* is translated as **u**

      U fazzu.   *I do so.*
      U cridi.   *He thinks so.*
      U d*i*cinu   *They say so.*

113

Comparison

Adverbs are compared like adjectives.

1. Regular:

> **granni** , *large;* **chiù granni** , *larger;*
> **u chiù granni** , *the largest*
>
> **nicu** , *small;* **chiù nicu** , *smaller*
> **u chiù nicu** , *the smallest*

2. Irregular:

> **bonu** , *well;* **megghiu** , *better;* **u megghiu** , *the best*
> **malu,** *bad;* **peggiu** , *worse;* **u peggiu** , *the worst*

Sì, no, còmu

Yes is **sì** . *No* is **no** . *What?* meaning *what do you say?* is **còmu ?**
Chi is often used to introduce questions.

> Pirchì unn rispunni? **Còmu? Chi** sì surdu?
> *Why don't you answer? What? Are you deaf?*

ESERCIZI: Translate the following into Sicilian:
1. His house is far. 2. He doesn't have any. 3. I can't see too well.
4. I'll go this evening. 5. Paulu is bigger than Ninu. 6. She is always good. 7. Four years ago. 8.What? Are you deaf? 9. He never speaks to me. 10. He'll go there tomorrow.

114

LEZZIONI DECIMA TAORMINA E CATANIA

Ninu: Maria, giacchì avemu sulu tri iorna prima di turnari in America unn putemu iri a Messina. Avemu giustu u tempu di pusari in Taormina e poi in Catania unna pigghiamu l'ariuplanu a Roma.

Maria: E di Roma un autru volu ê Stati Uniti.

Ninu: Dunca, in caminu a Taormina. *Vannu di San Fratello a Sant'Agata di Militello, poi a Milazzo e di Milazzo a Messina, un viaggiu di quasi tri ura.* U sai, Maria, avemu viaggiatu pir tri ura; ora semu nanticchia stanchi e è già menzu iornu. U sai chi ti dicu, pirchì unn truvamu un picculu ristoranti pir pranzari e ripusarni e doppu putemu cuntinuari u viaggiu a Taormina?

Maria: Pi' dir' a virità, mi pari un' idea splennenti; hai dovutu leggiri zaccu haiu in testa iustissa. Iamu. *Trovanu una trattturia unna mangianu un bel piattu di pasta fatta in casa cu sarsa di pumidamuri e furmaggiu duru messinisi grattugiatu, una bella insalata di lattuga,un sciaschicceddu di vinu russu imbuttigghiatu dâ Cooperativa Vinicula di Messina e poi una macedonia di frutta e un caffè espresso.*

Ninu: Ora mi sentu ristoratu e putemu cuntinuari u viaggiu a Taormina. *Doppu un ura e menzu arrivanu a Taormina unna si ospitanu in un albergu modestu. Passanu tuttu u pomeriggiu girannu i putii di Taormina.*

Maria: Mi piaci assai u ritrattu mosaicu chi accattai.

115

Ninu: Sì; tutti i putii vinninu articuli pî turisti, comu u ritrattu chi accattasti. Taormina è una bella città turistica; c'è un beddu teatru a l'apertu, u Teatro Greco; ma zaccu mi piaci sopratuttu sunnu i sciuri chi ornanu tutti i strati.

Maria: Ora vulissi far' una caminata na Via Luigi Pirandello, in onuri dô Laureatu Nobel, o chiù rinomatu scritturi sicilianu di stu seculu.

Ninu: Iamu. Senti, a prossima vota chi vinemu â Sicilia duvemu visitari Agrigentu,unna nasciu Pirandello.

Maria: Sì, facemu accussì, ma pir ora facemu a caminata.

Ninu: E doppu partemu pi' Catania.
Doppu dui ora di viaggiu arrivanu a granni città di Catania, unna trovanu un albergu modestu.
Maria, dumani facemu un giru di Catania e doppu dumani partenza pi Roma.
U iornu doppu.
U sai, Maria, i quattru nomi i chiù importanti in Catania sunnu, prima, Sant'Agata, a martira e santa patruna di Catania; secunnu, l'Etna, u vulcanu u chiù auitu di Europa, chi domina a città; terzu, Bellini, u gran composituri di *Norma* e autri operi; e quartu, l'Università di Catania, una dî dui importanti sedi intellettuali dâ Sicilia.

Maria: Voli diri chi, siccomu unn avemu troppu tempu, devemu visitari i località cu sti nomi.

Ninu: Brava, Maria. Prima di tuttu, iamu a visitari a Chiesa di Sant'Agata, e vicinu dâ chiesa,u Teatru Bellini e u Museu Bellinianu; e puru vicinu dâ chiesa l' Università di Catania.

116

Maria: E l'Etna?

Ninu: Ma certu. Pigghiamu a Ferrovia Circumetnea pir una vista dramatica dô vulcanu e i paiseddi intornu. E quannu turnamu, iemu direttamenti ô ariuportu, unna lassamu a machina e pigghiamu l'ariuplanu a Roma.

Maria: Sì, ma prima di imbarcari, vogghiu mangiari un piattu dî Spaghetti alla Norma, a rinomata pitanza catanisi.

Ninu: Ma certu, ntô ristoranti di l'ariuportu.

Maria: E poi, addiu â bedda Sicilia.

Tutti i dui: Addiu, bedda Sicilia!

117

LESSON TEN   TAORMINA AND CATANIA

Ninu: Maria, since we have only three days before returning home, we cannot visit Messina. We have just enough time to stop off in Taormina and then in Catania, where we'll catch a plane to Rome.

Maria: And from Rome, another flight to the States.

Ninu: So, on our way to Taormina. *They go from San Fratello to Sant'Agata di Militello, then to Milazzo and from Milazzo to Messina, a trip of about three hours.* You know, Maria, we've been travelling for three hours; we're a bit tired and it's already noon. I tell you, why don't we find a small restaurant, where we can have lunch and rest and then continue our trip to Taormina.

Maria: To tell you the truth, that sounds like a wonderful idea; you must have read just what I had in mind. So, let's go. *They find a small restaurant where they eat homemade pasta with tomato sauce and grated hard Messina cheese, a fine lettuce salad, a flask of red wine bottled by the Wine Cooperative of Messina, then a fruit salad and an espresso coffee.*

Ninu: Now I feel restored and we can continue our trip to Taormina. *After an hour and a half's travel, they arrive in Taormina, where they put up at an inexpensive hotel. They spend the afternoon visiting the Taormina shops.*

Maria: I like this framed mosaic I bought.

Ninu: Yes, all the shops sell touristy articles, like the frame you bought. Taormina is a beautiful tourist's city.It has a fine open air theater, the Greek Theater, but what I like above all are the flowers one finds along the streets.

Maria: I'd like to take a walk down the Via Luigi Pirandello, in honor of the Nobel Laureate, the most renowned Sicilian author of this century.

Ninu: Let's go. Listen, the next time we come to Sicily, we must visit Agrigento, where Pirandello was born.

Maria: Yes, let's do that, but right now, let's take the walk.

Ninu: And then we'll leave for Catania.
Two hours later, they arrive at the big city, Catania, where they find an inexpensive hotel.
Maria, tomorrow we'll tour Catania and the following day, we'll leave for Rome.
The following day.
You know, Maria, the four most important names in Catania are, first, Saint Agatha, the martyr and patron saint of Catania; secondly, Etna, the hightest volcano in Europe, which dominates the city; third, Bellini, the great composer of *Norma* and other operas;and fourth, The University of Catania, one of the two important intellectual seats of learning in Sicily.

Maria: That means that, since we do not have much time left, we must visit the places with those names.

119

Ninu: Very good, Maria. First of all, we'll go visit the Church of Saint Agatha, and, near the church, the Bellini Theater and the Bellini Museum; and, also near the church, the University of Catania.

Maria: And how about Etna?

Ninu: Of course. We'll take the Circumetnea Railroad for a dramatic view of the volcano and the surrounding towns. And when we return, we'll go directly to the airport, where we'll return the car and take the plane to Rome.

Maria: Yes, but before boarding, I want to eat a dish of Spaghetti alla Norma, the famous Catanian delicacy.

Ninu: But of course, at the airport restaurant.

Maria: And then, good bye to beautiful Sicily.

Both: Good bye, beautiful Sicily!

VOCABULARY

accatai	I bought
accattasti	you bought
addiu	good bye
apertu	open
artículi	articles
assai	a lot
*au*itu (AH wee too)	high
*au*tri	other
beddu	beautiful
bel	fine, beautiful
brava	good for you
caffè espresso	espresso coffee
caminata	walk
casa	house
cità	city
composituri	composer
cooperativa	cooperative
dicu	I say
dâ	by the
direttamenti	directly
domina	dominates
dramatica	dramatic
dunca	well then
duru	hard
duvemu	we must
ê	to the
fatta	made
furmaggiu	cheese
giacchì	since
giustu	just enough

granni	big
grattugiatu	grated
imbarcari	to board
imbuttigghiatu	bottled
importanti	important
insalata	salad
intellettuali	intellectual
intornu	near by
iri	to go
lassamu	we leave
lattuga	lettuce
leggiri	to read
località	places
macedonia di frutta	fruit salad
machina	car, auto
mangianu	they eat
martira	martyr
menzu	half
messinisi	Messinan
mosaicu	mosaic
nanticchia	a bit, somewhat
nasciu	was born
nomi	names
onuri	honor
operi	operas
ornanu	adorn
ospitanu	stay (at a hotel)
paiseddi	towns
pari	it seems
partemu	we leave
partenza	departure
passanu	they spend
patruna	patron

pî	for the
piaci	I like
piattu	dish
poi	then
prossima	next
pumidamuri (love apple)	tomatoes
pusari	pause, stop
putemu	we can
quannu	when
quasi	almost
rinomatu	famous
ripusarni	rest ourselves
ristoratu	restored
ritrattu	picture, frame
russu	red
sai	you know
santa	saint
sarsa	sauce
sciaschicceddu (shah kee CHEY doo)	small flask
sciuri (SHOO ree)	flowers
scritturi	writer, author
seculu	century
sedi	seats
semu	we are
senti	look, listen
sentu	I feel
siccomu	since
sopratuttu	above all
splennenti	brilliant
stanchi	tired (pl)
stissa	myself (fem)
strati	streets
sulu	only

teatru	theater
tempu	time
testa	head
tratttur/a	small restaurant
trovanu	they find
turisti	tourists
turnari	return
viaggiu	trip
vicinu	near
vinemu	we come
vin/cula	wine (adj)
v/nninu	they sell
vinu	wine
virità	truth
visitari	visit
vista	view
volu	flight
vota	time
vulcanu	volcano
zaccu (TSAH koo)	what

LOCUZIONI

EXPRESSIONS

prima di turnari	before returning
giustu u tempu	just enough time
u sai?	do you know?
è già	it's already
menzu iornu	noon
u sai chi ti dicu?	do you know what I think ?
pi' dir' a virità	to tell you the truth
un' idea splennenti	a wonderful idea
ora semu nanticchia stanchi	now we're a bit tired
è già menzu iornu	it's already noon

124

zaccu haiu in testa	what I've been thinking
iu stissa	I myself
fatta in casa	homemade
cu sarsa di pumidamuri	with tomato sauce
vinu russu	red wine
teatru a l'apertu	open-air theater
vulissi far' una caminata	I'd like to take a walk
a prossima vota	the next time
doppu dumani	day after tomorrow
fari una caminata	take a walk
u iornu doppu	the following day
u vulcanu u chiù *au*itu	the highest volcano
voli diri chi	it means that
prima di tuttu	first of all
prima di imbarcari	before boarding
a rinomata pitanza catanisi	the famous Catanian dish
addiu, bedda Sicilia	good bye beautiful Sicily
tutti i dui	both of them

ESERCIZI

EXERCISES

1. Copy the text, read it aloud and translate it.

2. Make up sentences with the following phrases and repeat them three times:
pi' dir' a virità; ora semu nanticchia stanchi; fatta in casa; prima di imbarcari

3. Translate into Sicilian:
just enough time; good bye beautiful Catania; do you know what I think ?; to tell you the truth; it's already noon

4. Translate into English:
vulissi far' una caminata; a rinomata pitanza catanisi; tutti i dui ;
prima di imbarcari; un' idea splennenti

5. Memorize:
u sai chi ti dicu?; a rinomata pitanza catanisi; ora semu nanticchia
stanchi; giustu u tempu; pi' dir' a virità

X. The Verb System

Like Italian, Sicilian has three conjugations: I -*ari*; II - *iriri*; III - *iri*. But it has fewer tenses than Italian. These are: present indicative, imperfect, preterite, present perfect, pluperfect, imperfect subjunctive, and past perfect subjunctive. It has present and past participles, but no passive, as there is in Italian. There is no present or present perfect subjunctive; the present subjunctive is replaced by the present indicative.Note that it has no future or conditional The vivid present (I do it tomorrow *for* I shall do it tomorrow) is used to indicate future, while the imperfect subjunctive takes the place of the conditional.

In the closing years of this century, however, because of the widespread use of Italian, many Sicilians have adopted the Italian future and conditonal as well as the present subjunctive.

See the Appendix for the irregular verbs. This section offers a simplified and reduced presentation.

Auxiliary Verb

Unlike Italian, which has two auxiliary verbs,*avere* and *essere*, Sicilian has only one, *aviri*. *Essiri* is like any other verb of the second conjugation and is inflected accordingly. The regular endings in the verbs that follow are preceded by a hyphen (-) after the stem.

Aviri , *to have*

Infinitive	Present participle	Past participle
av-iri	av-ennu	av-utu

127

Present Indicative		Imperfect		Preterite	
I have, etc.		*I had, was having,etc.*		*I had, etc.*	
h*a*iu	avemu	av-eva	av-*e*vamu	appi	*a*ppimu
h*a*i	aviti	av-evi	av-*e*vu [-vavu]	avisti	av*i*stivu
havi	hannu	av-eva	av-*e*vanu	appi	*a*ppiru

Imperative: The auxiliary has a negative imperative, but no positive.
The infinitive is used for this form:

Unn **avir'** paura. *Have no fear.*

Future: vivid present   Conditional: imperfect subjunctive

128

The Regular Verbs

First Conjugation -ari

Parrari, *to speak*

Infinitive	Present participle	Past participle
parr-ari	parr-annu	parr-atu

Present Indicative *I speak, etc.*		Imperfect *I used to speak, etc.*		Preterite *I spoke, etc.*	
parr-u	parr-amu	parr-ava	parr-avamu	parr-ai	parr-ammu
parr-i	parr-ati	parr-avi	parr-avavu	parr-asti	parr-astivu
parr-a	parr-anu	parr-ava	parr-avanu	parr-ò	parr-aru

Imperative: positive - parra (tu), *speak*, parramu, *let us speak*
parrati (vui), *speak*
negative - unn parrari, *don't speak*, etc.

Future: vivid present

Ci parru dumani (I speak to him tomorrow)
I'll speak to him tomorrow

Quannu veni? (When does he come?)
When will he come?

Second Conjugation - *idiri*

This conjugation includes verbs whose infinitives have the stress on the third syllable from the end - the antepenult.

Cr*i*diri, *to believe*

Infinitive	Present participle	Past participle
cr*i*d-iri	crid-ennu	crid-utu

Present Indicative	Imperfect	Preterite
I believe, etc.	*I used to believe, etc.*	*I believed, etc.*

crid-u	crid-emu	crid-iva	crid-*i*vamu	crid-*i*i	crid-immu
crid-i	crid-iti	crid-ivi	crid-*i*vavu	crid-*i*sti	crid-*i*stivu
crid-i	cr*i*d-inu	crid-iva	crid-*i*vanu	crid-*i*u	crid-iru

Imperative: positive - cridi, *believe,* criditi, cridemu

negative - unn cr*i*diri, *don't believe,* unn criditi, unn cridemu

Future: vivid present

Ci cridu quann'u vidu (I believe it when I see him.)
I'll believe it when I see him.

Third Conjugation - *iri*

Partiri, *to leave, depart*

Infinitive	Present participle	Past participle
part-iri	part-ennu	par-titu

Present Indicative		Imperfect		Preterite	
I depart, etc.		*I used to depart, etc.*		*I departed, etc.*	
part-u	part-emu	part-iva	part-*i*vamu	part-*i*i	part-immu
part-i	part-iti	part-ivi	par-*i*vavu	part-*i*sti	part-*i*stivu
part-i	part-inu	part-iva	part-*i*vanu	part-*i*u	part-iru

Imperative: positive - parti, *leave,* partiti, partemu
negative - unn partiri, *don't leave,* unn partiti, unn partemu

Future: vivid present

U vidu dumani
I'll see him tomorrow.

Finiri, *to finish*

As in Italian, the third conjugation has a number of verbs whose stem changes in the first, second and third singular and the third plural of the present indicative and in the second person singular of the positive imperative. These are:

finiri, *to finish*	**capiri** *,to understand*
puliri, *to clean*	**preferiri** , to *prefer.*

Finiri is conjugated as follows:

Present Indicative		Imperative	
fini-sciu	fin-emu	positive	fin-isci, *finish,*
fini-sci	fin-iti		fin-iti, fin-emu
fin-isci	fin-*i*scinu	negative	unn finiri, *don't finish,* etc

Irregular Verbs

See the Appendix for a complete treatment

Note the following uses of verbs:

1. When used as the subject, or direct object of a verb, the English gerund(ending in *-ing*) is rendered in Sicilian by the *infinitive*.

Mi piaci <u>viaggiari</u>	*I like travelling*
Odiu <u>studiari</u>	*I hate studying*

2. The English gerund preceded by a preposition (and followed by an infinitive) is translated as follows:

di, *of—* **inveci di**, *instead of—***senza** , *without—*
doppu di, *after—***prima di**, *before*

U viziu **di fumari**.	*The habit **of** smoking.*
Doppu di parrari...	***After** speaking...*
Inveci di criticari...	***Instead of** criticizing...*
Prima di muriri...	***Before** dying...*
P**a**rranu **senza** pensari.	*They speak **without** thinking.*

3. After **fari**, *to make* or *to have (i.e. to cause)*, **sentiri** , *to hear,* and **v***i***diri**, to see, Sicilian uses the infinitive to express an English past participle.

Si fa **capiri**.	*He makes himself <u>understood</u>.*
Fazzu **fari** un paru di scarpi.	*I shall have a pair of shoes <u>made</u>.*
Sentu **diri**..	*I hear it <u>said</u> ...*
U visti **ammazzari**.	*I saw him <u>killed</u>*

4. After **lassari** , *to let,* and often after the preposition **da**, a Sicilian active infinitive is used to translate a passive one in English.

  Si lassa **ingannari.**   *He lets himslf be deceived.*
  Unn c'è nenti da **fari.**   *There is nothing to be done.*

5. When used as an adjective, the past participle is inflected like any other adjective.

        Sti vasi sunnu **rutti**.   *These vases are broken.*

6. In negative commands, the infinitive is always used instead of the second person singular of the imperative.

            F**a**llu. *Do it.*
        Unn u **fari**. *Don't do it.*

7. The imperfect denotes a continuing action, while the preterite is used to describe an action that has been completed.

Tras*i*u mentri **dorm** *i***vamu.** *He entered while we were sleeping.*
U **fici** l'annu passatu.   *He did it last year.*

ESERCIZI:

A. Conjugate (a) **parrari,** *I speak, you speak, etc.*(b) **cridiri** and (c) **partiri** in the present indicative.

B. Translate the following into Sicilian:
1. I am afraid. 2. Do it today. 3. I make myself understood.
4. I hear it said that he speaks well. 5. I like studying. 6. I'll finish it tomorrow. 7. Instead of criticizing, do it. 8. Don't let yourself be deceived. 9. He makes himself understood. 10. He speaks without thinking.

134

KEY TO EXERCISES

Lesson 1

2. Unna iemu pi pigghiari l'ariuplanu â Sicilia?
Fra un ura. Quannu è u prossimu volu? Iti â destra.

3. Look. I'll reserve two seats for you. Let's go, Maria.
Excuse me.

Grammar Section

1. Ninu Mondello è un bon medicu. 2. Anna Mondello è prufisuri
di inglisi. 3. Gianni è un bon pueta.

Lesson 2

3. Permettitimi di prisintarmi. Nascemmu in America.
Milli grazii. Vuautri, siti Siciliani?

4. Here is my telephone number. We have visited relatives in
America. Come and spend one or two days with us. Happy to
meet you.

Grammar Section

1. Un paru di ova. 2. Ninu e Gianni sunnu amici. 3. Cintinara di
migghia. 4. I medici nun sunnu siciliani; sunnu greci. 5. I frati
sunnu colleghi.

Lesson 3

3. Si pò accattari qualsiasi tipu di mangiari nâ Vucciria. Dumani
putemu fari un giru di Palermo in autobus. Comu si chiama u
nostru albergu?

4. Isn't it true that the Pretoria is a modestly priced hotel?
We have a beautiful room with shower. Today we can use the

tickets we bought yesterday.

Grammar Section
1. Paulu è u frati maggiuri. 2.Ninu è chiù nicu di Paulu.
3. Sta stanza è a chiù granni.

Lesson 4
3. u nostru lettu è commudu; vogghiu pruvari u bar cca vicinu;
oggi u giru è a pedi; iu prefirisciu lavarmi na vasca du bagna.

4. don't you think it's a reasonable price? I prefer bathing ina
bathtub; I prefer the shower; let's do just that.

Grammar Section
1. Chiamanu a Paulu manazza. 2. A stanza è larghissima.
3. Pippinuzzu è frati di Turiddu.

Lesson 5
3. dda putemu mangiari pisci frischi; iti â sinistra; dda putemu
truvari un ristoranti; unna è l'università?

4. but first we must ask for directions; can you tell me how to get
to the Corso Vittorio Emanuele? there's a statue in every corner; I
am tired and hungry

Grammar Section
1. Una trentina di casi 2. Dui para di scarpi 3. Pippinuzza havi dui
duzzini di libri. 4. Sunu i quattru e menzu. 5. Sei di maggiu.
6. Dumila centu.

Lesson 6
3. Iamuninni!; vulemu mangiari pitanzi siciliani; Racumannu a
pitanza speciali di Palermo; u camareri ci duna a lista.

4. the lovely Sicilian bread; a tip for the waiter ; what do you recommend?; a table for two.

Grammar Section

1. Ni vistimu 2. U fa pir mia. 3. Dammilu. 4. Unn u vogghiu.
5. Vili duna. 6. Ni vuliti? 7. Carlu mi duna u libbru.
8. Si vesti. 9. Iddi parranu.

Lesson 7

3. Ninu, sempri chi scherzi; quannu pozzu viniri pir un' ondulazioni permanenti?; mi sta beni; nescinu dô negozziu.

4. a stylish dress; may I try it on?; a beauty parlor; a bottle of mouthwash.

Grammar Section

1. Nostra figghia è bedda 2. Stu libbru è u sò 3. L'omu a cui parru. 4. Cu parra? 5. Da fimmina è bedda. 6. Nostra matri e a sò.
7.Quantu soldi custa? 8.A cu vidi? 9. Chistu è bonu.

Lesson 8

3. fattu apposta pî turisti ; un beddu paiseddu; duvemu pagariuna tassa di cincu dollari; doppu un ura di viaggiu.

4. three hundred and fifty dollars a week; I have an international driver's license; even gasoline is expensive; butit's worthwhile, don't you think?

Grammar Section

1.Ni havi? 2.Unn sapi zaccu fari. 3. Arrivò da Roma oggi.
4.Fu fattu da Maria. 5. Nostra matri e a sò. 6.Quantu custa?
7.A cu vidi? 8.Chista è bona. 9.Unn havi nenti da fari.

137

Lesson 9

3. chi sapuri incantevuli; un paiseddu pitturiscu; un caminu chi gira e gira; una pendenza panoramica; una pitanza tipica di sti parti.

4. willingly; we begin the climb; they chased out; it almost makes one's head spin; he hands a bouquet of flowers.

Grammar Section

1. A so casa è luntanu. 2.Unn ni havi. 3. Unn pozzu vidiri troppu bonu. 4. Ci vaiu stasira. 5. Paulu è chiù granni di Ninu. 6. Idda è sempri bona. 7. Quattru anni fa. 8. Còmu? Chi sì surdu? 9. Non mi parra mai. 10. Ci va dumani.

Lesson 10

3. giustu u tempu; addiu bedda Catania; u sai chi dicu ?; pi' dir'a virità; è già menzu iornu

4. I want to take a walk; the famous Catanian dish; both of them; before boarding; a brilliant idea

Grammar Section

B.1. Haiu paura. 2. Fallu oggi. 3. Mi fazzu capiri. 4. Sentu diri chi parra bonu. 5. Mi piaci studiari. 6. U finisciu dumani.
7. Inveci di criticari, fallu. 8. Unn ti lassari ingannari. 9. Si fa capiri.10. Parra senza pinsari.

138

APPENDIX

The Irregular Verbs

First Conjugation -*ari*

The following irregular verbs belong to the first conjugation:
d*a*ri, f*a*ri, st*a*ri. The irregular forms (paradigms) are underlined.

d*a*ri,
to give, is irregular in the present indicative and the preterite.
All the other tenses are regular.

Infinitive: da-ri   Present participle: da-nnu   Past participle: da-tu

Present Indicative		Preterite	
I give, etc.		*I gave, etc.*	
dugn-u	da-mu	de-tti	de-ttimu
dun-i	da-ti	da-sti	d*a*-stivu
dun-a	da-nnu	de-tti	de-ttiru

f*a*ri, *to do,* is irregular in the present participle, the present
indicative, the imperfect, the imperfect subjunctive, and the preterite,
all of which use the stem of the obsolete alternate, **fac*i*ri.** All the
other tenses are regular.

Infinitive: fa-ri   Present participle: fac-ennu   Past participle: fa-ttu

Present Indicative
I do, etc.
fa-zzu[facciu]fac-emu
fa-i   fac-iti

139

stari, *to stay, to be, to remain,* is irregular in the present indicative and the preterite. All the other tenses are regular. The second person singular of the positive imperative drops the final i, sta'

Infinitive: sta-ri   Present participle: sta-nnu   Past participle: sta-tu

Present Indicative
I stay, etc.

sta-iu	sta-mu
sta-i	sta-ti
sta	sta-nnu

Second Conjugation - *idiri*

essiri , *to be,* is irregular in the participles, the present indicative, the imperfect, the preterite and the imperfect subjunctive.

Infinitive: ess-iri   Present participle: se-nnu   Past participle: sta-tu

Present Indicative
I am, etc.

su-gnu	se-mu
sì	s-iti
è	su-nu

mettiri, *to put, to place* is irregular in the preterite. There is a change in stem in the participles mittennu, mittutu, but also

140

mettennu,etc. and in the imperfect, similarly **mi**ttiva or **me**ttiva, etc.

Preterite: mi-si, mitt-isti, mi-si, mit-emmu, mitt-istivu, mitt-eru
[mi-seru]

perdiri, t*o lose,* is irregular in the present indicative, in which the
stem changes to **pird-** in the first and second persons plural:
per-du, per-di, per-di, **pir-** demu, **pir-** diti, per-dinu.

v*i*diri, t*o see,* is irregular in the past participle,**vistu** [or **vidutu**],
and in the first person singular and third persons singular and plural
of the preterite:
visti [vitti], vidisti, visti [vitti, vidiu], videmmu, vidistivu, videru,
[vistiru]

Third Conjugation - *i*ri

aviri , see auxiliary, above

duviri [**doviri**], *to have to, must, ought,* is irregular in the
participles and the present indicative. Note the mixture of both
infinite stems.
Infinitive: duv-iri   Present participle: dov-ennu   Past participle: dov-utu
                                    [duv-ennu]   [duv-utu]

Present Indicative
I have to, etc.

dev-u   duv-emu
dev-i   duv-iti
dev-i   dev-inu

íri, *to go*, is irregular in the participles, the present indicative, the preterite, and the imperfect subjunctive.

<u>Infinitive:</u> **í**r-i   <u>Present participle:</u> ie-nnu   <u>Past participle:</u> i-utu

<u>Present Indicative</u>
I go, etc.

<u>v**a**-iu</u> <u>ie-mu</u>
<u>va-i</u>   <u>i-ti</u>
<u>va</u>   <u>va-nnu</u>

muriri, *to die*, is irregular in the past participle (**mortu**) and the present indicative, in which the stem changes to **mor-** in the first, second and third persons singular and the third person plural.

<u>Present Indicative:</u> **mor-** u, **mor-** i, **mor-** i, mur-emu, mur-iti, **m**o**r-**inu

putiri , *to be able to,* is irregular in the present indicative, and the preterite.

<u>Present Indicative:</u>
I can, etc.
<u>po-zzu</u> put-emo
<u>po-i</u>   put-iti
<u>pò</u>   <u>po-nnu</u>

sapiri , *to know*, is irregular in the present indicative and the preterite.

<u>Present Indicative:</u>
I know, etc.
<u>sacci-u</u> sap-emo

142

sa-i   sap-iti
sap-i   sa-nnu

ten*i*ri [t**e**ni**ri, tiniri**] , *to keep, to hold,* is irregular in the present indicative, and the preterite.

Infinitive: ten- *i*ri   Present participle: ten- **e**nnu   Past participle: ten-***u***tu

Present Indicative
I hold, etc.

tegn-u	tin-emu
te-ni	tin-iti
te-ni	ten-inu

ven *i*ri [v**e**ni**ri, viniri**] , *to come,* is irregular in the present indicative, and the preterite and is conjugated like **ten *i*ri** [t**e**ni**ri, tiniri**] .

vul *i*ri, *to wish, to want,* is irregular in the present indicative.

Infinitive: vul-iri   Present participle: vul-ennu   Past participle: vul-utu

Present Indicative
I wish, etc.

v**o**gghi-u	vul-emu
vo-i	vul-iti
vol-i	vo-nnu

143

SICILIAN-ENGLISH VOCABULARY

A

a, [la], *f., sing.* **i**, **li**, *pl.*, the
a, *prep.*, to,at
â , to the
abbacu, *n.m.*, abacus
accattai , *1st s. pret. of*
  accattari, to buy
accattammu *1st pl.. pret. of*
  accattari, to buy
accantu a, *prep.,* along,by
accuminciari , *vb.,* to begin
accussì bonu , *adv. expr.* so
  well
acchianata , *n. f.*,climb
acqua, *n. f.*, water;— **denti-**
  fricia , mouthwash
addìu, *inter.*, good bye
affari , *n.m.*, affair,business
affinchè , *conj.*, in order that
affumicatu , *adj.*, smoked
aieri [ieri],*adv.*, yesterday
aierisira , *adv.*, last night
albergaturi , *n.m.*,hotelier
albergu , *n.m.*, hotel
alcuni , *adj.*, some
allura , *adv.*,then
altrimenti, *conj.*,or else
ammazzari, *vb.*, to kill
amicu , *n.m.*, friend

amu, *1st s.pres. ind.of* **amari**,
  to love
anchi , *conj.*, also, too
aneddu , *n.m.*, ring
angilu , *m.*,angel
annu, *n.m*, year
anticu , *n.m.*,old, ancient
anzi , *conj.*, rather
aperitìvu , *n.m.*, aperitif
apertu, *past p.* **apriri**,
  to open
apposta , *adv.*, on purpose
aprili, *n.m.*, april
aranci, *n.m.*,oranges
ariuportu , *n.m.*, airport
arrivammu *1st pl, pret..of*
  arrivari, to arrive
arrivanu *3d pl, pres.ind..of*
  arrivari, to arrive
arrivata, *n. f.*, arrival
arrivò, *3d s. pret.of* **arrivari**,
  to arrive
arrizzitatu , *adj.*, settled in
artìculu , *n.m.*, article
aspirina , *n. f.*, aspirin
assai , *adv.*, a lot
assittatu , *adj.*, seated
attimu, *n.m.*, instant
autobus , *n.m.*, bus

auitu (AHW wee too), *n.m.*,
high

autostrata , *n. f.*, road,
highway

autri, *pron.*, others

autru (**-a**), *adj., pron.*,
other

avantaieri , *adv.*, day before
yesterday

avanti , *adv. prep.*,forward!

avemu , *1st pl.pres. ind.of*
aviri, to have

aviri, *vb.*, to have

azioni , *n. f.*,action

B

bar, *n.m...*, coffee shop

beddu -a *adj.*, pretty

bellu[bel] , *adj.*, fine

benchì , *conj.*, although

beni , *adv.*, well

benissimu , *adv.*, very
good,fine

benzina , *n. f.*, gasoline

biancu , *adj.*,white

biglietti , *n.m* tickets

bisogna , *3d sing.* to be
necessary

blu , *adj.*, blue

bizantini , *adj.*, Byzantine

bon' (**-u** ,**-a**), *adj.*, good

bracciu [brazzu], *n.m,(*pl.-**a**)
arm

bravu , *adj.*, able, skilful, *inter.*
good for you!

brindisi , *n.m,* toast

bruttiredda , *pron.*, somewhat
ugly

bruttu, *adj.*, ugly, bad

burru, *n.m.*, butter

buccazza , *n. f.*, big mouth

buccuncinu , *n.m.*, a mouthful,
the sweet-ricotta-filled
pastry.

buttigghia , *n. f.*, bottle

C

cacciatu , *p. part of* **cacciari** ,
to chase

caffè , *n.m.*,coffee

caffè espresso , *n.m.*,
espresso coffee

cammara dî ospiti , *n.m.*,
guest room

camareri, *n.m.*, waiter

caminata , *n. f.*, walk

caminu (in) ,*adv. phrase*, on
the road

Canadà, *n.m.*, Canada

cani , *n.m.*, dog

cantu , *n.m.*,corner

canusci , *3d s.pres.ind.of*
can usciri , to know

can usciri , *vb,* to know, get to
know

capiri , *vb,* to understand

capisciu *1st sing.pres. ind.* **capiri**, to understand

cappuccinu, *n.m.*, cappuccino

caru, *adj.*, dear, expensive

Carlu, *n.m.*, Charles

carni, *n.m.*, meat

carta, *n.f.*, map

casa, *n.f.*, house

cascieri, *n.m.*, cashier

casicedda, *n.f.*, small house

cast igu, *n.m.*, punishment

casu, *conj.*, in case

cattedrali, *n.f.*, cathedral

cca, *adv.*, here

c'è, there is

cena, *n.f.*, dinner

centrali, *adj.*, central, main

certu, *adj.*, certain, of course

chi, *adv.*, than, *conj.*, than, that, *pron.*, what

chî (cu+i) *prep.phrase*, with the

chiama, *3d s. pres.ind.of* **chiamari**, to call

chiamanu, *3d pl. pres.ind.of* **chiamari**, to call

chiamari, *vb.*, to call

chiamarisi, *vb.*, to be called

chiamati, *1st pl. pres.ind.of* **chiamari**, to call

chiamu, *1st s. pres.ind.of* **chiamari**, to call

chiamatu-a, *adj.*, called

chiaru, *adj.*, *adv.*, clear, clearly

chiaramenti, *adv.*, clearly

chiddu, *pron.,.m.*, that one

chiesa, *n.f.*, church

chiù, *adj.*, more

chissu, *pron.,.m.*, that one

chistu, *pron.,.m.*, this one

chiù, *adj.*, more

chi unqui, *pron.*, whoever

ci, *pron.*, to him, to her, to them; *adv.*, there

ciascunu, *pron.*, each, every

cincu, *adj.*, five

cintinaru, *n.m.*, hundred

città, *n.f.*, city

circa *(approx)*, *prep.*, about

coci, *3d s.of* **cociri**, to cook

colera, *n.m.*, cholera

collega, *n.m.*, colleague

commissa, *n.f.*, saleslady

comu, *adv*, how, like, *conj.*, as **còmu ?** *adv.*, what?

comu anchi, *conj.*, as well as

commudu, *adj.*, comfortable

composituri, *n.m.*, composer

contra, *prep.*, against

contu, *n.m.*, bill

cooperativa, *n.f.*, cooperative

coppia, *n.f.*, couple

cornettu, *n.m.*, filled croissant

cosa, *n.f.*, thing

costa, *n.f.*, coast

crema, *n. f.*, cream, — **di varva**, shaving cream
criatu, *adj.*, created
cridi *2d s. pres.ind.of* **cridiri**, to believe
criticari, *vb.*, to criticize
crucianu, *3d pl. pres.ind.of* **cruciari**, to cross
cu, *prep.*, with
cu, *pron.*, who, whom
cû, *prep.*, with the
cui, *pron.*, who, which
culazioni, *n. f.*, breakfast
cunserva, *n. f.*, preserve
cuntenti, *n.m.*, content, happy
cuntinuari, *vb.*, to continue
cuntò, *3d s. pret.* **cuntari**, to count
cuntorni, *n.m.*, side-dish
cupula, *n. f.*, cupola
cursa, *n. f.*, (taxi) run
curtu, *adj.*, short
custa, *3d s. pres.ind.of* **custari**, to cost

D

da, *prep.*, from
dâ, *prep.*, by the
dachì, *conj.*, since (temporal)
dari, *vb.*, to give
darreri, *prep.*, behind
datu chi, *conj.*, granting that
davanti a, *prep.*, before (place), in front of

daveru, *adv.*, indeed, really
dda, *adv.*, there
ddocu, *adv.*, there
decina, *n. f.*, about ten
destra, *adv.*, right (side)
determinazioni, *n. f.*, determination
detti, *3d s. pret of* **dari**, to give
devi, *3d s. pres.ind.of* **duviri**, to have to, must, ought
di, *prep.*, of
dialettu, *n.m.*, dialect
dichiarari, *vb.*, to declare
dicinu, *3d pl. pres.ind.of* **diri**, to say
difettu, *n.m.*, fault, defect
differenti, *adj.*, different
deliziusu, *adj.*, delicious
dinocchiu, *n.m.*, (pl.-a) knee
dintra di, *prep.*, inside of
direttamenti, *adv.*, directly
diri, *vb.*, to say, to tell
dirrimpettu, *prep.*, opposite
discretu, *pron.*, modest, reasonable
dissi, *3d s. pret. of* **diri**, to tell
domina, *3d s. pres. ind.* **dominari**, to dominate
domu, *n.m.*, dome, cathedral
doppu, *prep.*, after
doppu chi, *conj.*, after
doppu dumani, *adv.*, day after tomorrow

dramaticu, *adj.*,dramatic
du, *adj.,m.*, that
duccia, *n. f.*, shower
dugana, *n. f.*,customs
dui, *adj.*, two
dummanari, *vb.*, to ask (for)
dumani, *adv.*, tomorrow
duna, *3d s. pres.ind.of* **dari**,
   to give
dunca, *conj.*, then, (**però**,
   perciò, therefore)
duranti, *prep.*,during
duru, *adj.*, hard
duviri, *vb.*, to have to
duzzina, *n.m.*, dozen

E

e, *conj.*,and
è, *3d s. pres.ind.of* **essiri**, to be
ê, *prep.*, to the (pl)
eccettu, *prep.*,except
eccettu chi, *conj.*, unless
eccu, *adv.*, here is, are
eleganti, *n.m.*,stylish
ê novi, *prep. phrase*, at nine
   o'clock
entrammi, *pron., adj.*,both
essiri, *vb.*, to be

F

fa, *adv*, ago
facemu, *1st, pl.., pres. ind.*
   fari, to do
faci[fa], *3d sing., pres. ind.*
   fari, to do

facili, *adj.*, easy
fami, *n.m.*,hungry, hunger
famigghia, *n. f.*, family
fari, *vb.*, to do
farmacia, *n. f.*, drug store
farmacista, *n.m.*, pharmacist
fattu, *adj.*, made, *n.m.*, fact
favuri, *n.m.*, favor, **pir f.**,
   please
fazzu, *1st s. pres.ind.of* **fari**,
   to do
felici, *adj.*, happy
ficu, *n.m.*, fig tree
ficu, *n. f.*, fig
figghiu, *n.m.*, son
Filippu, *n.m.*, Philip
fimmina, *n. f.*, woman
fina, *prep.*, as far as
finchì, *conj.*, until
finiri, *vb.*, to finish
finitu, *past part.* **finiri**, to
   finish; *adj.*
finocchiu, *n.m.*, fennel
finu a, *prep.*, up to
fisiologu, *n.m.*, physiologist
fora, *adv.*, outside
fora di, *prep.*, outside of,
   out of
forsi, *adv.*, perhaps
fra, *prep.*, among, between,
   within
francamenti, *adv.*, frankly

francisi , *n.m.*, *adj.*, *pron.*
French
francu , *adv.*, frank
frati , *n.m.*, brother
friscu-a , *adj.*, fresh
friscu, friscu , *adj. phrase*,
quite fresh
frittu , *adj.*, fried
fruttu , *n.m.*,(pl.-a) *fruit*
fuga , *n.f.*, flight
fumari , *vb.*, to smoke
fummu *1st, pl.., pret.* **essiri** to
be
funcia , *n.f.*, mushroom
furmaggiu , *n.m.*, cheese
furtizza , *n.f.*, fortress

G

gattu , *n.m.*, cat
gentilizza , *n.f.*, gentility
gentilissimu , *adj.*, very
gentle, very kind
gerenti , *n.m.*, manager
gestu , *n.m.*,gesture, sign
giacchì , *prep.*, as for,since
giardinu , *n.m.*, garden
girari , *vb.*, to tour
giru ,*n.m.*, tour
giustu , *adj.*, just right
gran(ni) ,[ranni], *adj.*,big,
great
grattugiatu , *adj.*, grated
grazzii , *inter.*, thanks

grecu , *n.m.*,Greek
gridu , *n.m.*, (pl.-a) shout
guancia , *n.f.*, cheek

H

haiu *1st s. pres.ind.of* **aviri** ,
to have
hannu, *3d pl. pres.ind.of*
aviri , to have

I

iamu, *1st pl. imp.* **iri,** to go
ieri [aieri] , *adv.*,yesterday
idea , *n.f.*, idea
iddu , *pron.*, he
iddi , *pron.*, they
íditu , *n.m.*, (pl.-a) finger
iemu, *1st pl. pres.ind.of* **iri**,to
go
i,li,l' , *m.,f., pl*, the
imbarcari , *vb.*, to board
imbuttigghiatu , *adj.*, bottled
imparari , *vb.*, to learn
impiegatu , *n.m.*, employee
importanti , *adj.*, important
in , *prep.*,in
incantevuli , *adj.*, enchanting
incontrati , *2d pl. pres.ind.of*
incontrari , to encounter
índica, *3d s. pres.ind.of*
indicari , to indicate
índicu , *n.m.*, indigo
ingannari ,*vb.*, to deceive
inglisi , *adj., pron.*, English
insalata , *n.f.*, salad

insigna *3d s. pres.ind.of*
  insignari , to teach
insignari , to teach
insumma , *adv.*, in short
intellettuali , *adj.*, intellectual
interessanti , *adj.*, interesting
internazionali , *adj.*,
  international
int*o*nacu , *n.m.*, plaster
intornu a , *prep.*,about
  (around)
intr*i*nsicu , *adj.*, intrinsic
inveci di , *prep.*, instead of
invitatu ,*adj.*, invited
iornata , *n.m.*, day
iornu (*pl*-a), *n.m.*, day (s)
iri, *vb.*, to go
iti, *2d pl.*, *imp.***iri**, to go
iu, *pron.*, I

L

labbru, *n.m.*,(pl.-a) lip
lagu , *n.m*, lake
largu ,*adj.*, wide
lastricu , *n.m*, pavement
latriceddu , *n.m*, something of
  a thief
lassari , *vb.*, to depart, let go
lassatu , *past p.* **lassari** , to
  leave, depart, let go
latti , *n.m*, milk
lattuga , *n. f.*, lettuce
latu , di...stu , *prep.*, on this
  side

lavarsi , *refl.vb*, to wash
  oneself
leggiri , *vb.*, to read
Lei, *pron.*,you (an Italian
  borrowing)
lettu , *n.m*,bed
lezzioni , *n. f.*, lesson
li , *pron.*, them
libbru , *n.m*, book
lignu , *n.m*,(pl.-a)wood
limuni , *n.m.s*, lemon tree
limuni , *n.m.pl.*, lemon
linii , *n.m*, lines
liri , *n.m*, liras
lista , *n. f.*, menu
littra , *n. f.*, letter
località , *n. f.*, place
longu , *adj.*, long
lungu , *adv.*, along
luntanu , *adv.*, distant, far.

M

ma, *conj.*, but
macedonia di frutta , *n.m.*,
  fruit salad
machina , *n. f.*, auto, car
macchina a vapuri , *n.m.*,
  steam engine
maggiu , *n.m.*, may
maggiuri , *adj.*, larger
maistà , *n.m.*, majesty
malu, *adj.*, *adv.*, bad
manazza , *n.m.*, big hands

mancanu, *3d pl. pres.ind.of*
 mancari, to lack
mancia, *n. f.*, tip
manicu, *n.m.*, handle
mangia, *3d s. pres.ind.of*
 mangiari, to eat
mangiari, *vb.*, to eat
manu, *n. f.*, hand
Mari Tirrenu, *n.m.*,
 Tyrrhenian Sea
Maria, *n. f.*, Mary
martira, *n. f.*, martyr
matri, *n. f.*, mother
mazzu, *n.m*, bunch, bouquet
me, mè, *adj., pron.*,my,mine
medicu, *n.m.*, doctor
megghiu, *adj., adv.*, better
membru, *n.m.*, (pl.-a) member
mentri, *conj.,* while
menu ,*adv., pron., adj.*, less
 a ... chi, *conj.,* unless
menzu, *adj.,* half
menzu, nu...di, *prep.,* in the
 midst of
menzu, pir...di, by means of
messinisi, *adj.,*Messinan
mettiri, *vb.,* to put
mi, *pron,* me, myself
mia, *pron.,* me
migghiaru, *n.m.*, thousand
migghiu, *n.m.*, mile
mila, *pron.,* thousand
milli, *adj.,* thousand

minsogna, *n. f.*, lie
minuri, *adj.,* smaller
minutu, *n.m.*, minute
mistu, *adj.,*mixed
mità, *n. f,* half
modu, di...chi (result),*conj.*
 so that
momentu, *n.m,* moment
monarca, *n.m,* monarch
mos aicu, *pron.,* mosaic
motivu, pir... di, *prep.,*
 because of
mugghieri, *n. f.*, wife
munita, *n. f.*, money
muriu, *3d s.pret. of* **muriri**, to
 die
muru, *n.m,* (pl.-a)wall
musaicu, *n.m,* mosaic

N

na (u-na), *indef. art.* a
nanticchia ,*adv.,* a bit,
 somewhat
nascemmu, *1st pl. pret. of*
 nasciri, to be born
nascinu, *3d pl. pres.ind.of*
 nasciri, to be born
nasciuti, *p.p.of* **nasciri,** to be
 born
nasuni, *n.m.,*bignose *nor*
nè, *conj.,* nor
nè...nè, *conj.,* neither...nor
neanchi, *conj.,* nor even
negozziu, *n.m.,* shop

nemicu , *n.m*, enemy
nenti, *pron.,* nothing
nent'autru , *pron.,* nothing else
neppuru , *conj.,* nor...either
nescinu , *3d pl. pres.ind.of* **nesciri** , to leave
nessunu , *pron.,* no one
ni, *pron.*of it. us, ourselves *adv.,* of it
niautri [nuautri] *pron.,* we
nicu , *adj.,* small
nomu , *n.m*, name
no , *adv.,* no
non , [**nun**] *adv.,* not
non ...chiù , *pron.,* no more
non ...mai, *adv.,* never
nonu ,*adj.,* ninth
nostru , *adj.,* our
notti , *n. f.,* night
ntâ (in+ a) , *prep.,* in the
nu, in the
nuautri [niautri ,nui], *pron.,* we
nuddu , *pron.,* no one
nuliggiu , *n.m.,* rental
nulla , nothing
numerusu , *pron., adj.,*many
numiru , *n.m.,* number
nun ,*adv.,* not
nundimenu , *conj.,nevertheless*

O

o , *conj.,* or
ô , *prep.,* to the
oca , *n. f.,* goose
odiari , *vb.,* to hate
offro , *n.m.,* offer
oggi , *adv.,* today
ogni , *adj.,* each, every
ognunu , *adj.,* each, every
oltri , *prep.,* besides (in addition to),beyond
omu , *n.m.,* man
ondulazioni , *n. f.,* wave;
    —permanenti, permanent
onnibus , *n.m.,* omnibus
onuri , *n.m.,* honor
opera , *n. f.,* opera
opuru , *conj.,* or
ora , *adv.,* now
ora ora , *adv.,* right away
ornari , *vb.,* to adorn
ospitu , *n.m.,* guest
ossu , *n.m., (pl.-a)*bone
osteria , *n.f.,* tavern
ovu , *n.m., egg*

P

pâ (pir+ a) , *prep.,* for the
pagari , *vb.,* to pay
paiseddu , *n.m.,* small town
paisi , *n.m.,* town

palla, *n. f.,* ball

palazzu, *n.m.*, palace, mansion

palermitanu, *pron.,*
Palermitan

pani, *n.m.*, bread

pani e cupertu, *nounal
phrase,* cover

panoramicu, *adj.,* panoramic

panuzzu, *n.m.*, (lovely)bread

parenti, *n.m.,* relatives

pari, *3d s.pres. ind. of* pariri,
to seem

paricchi, *adj.,* several

Parigi, *n.f.,* Paris

parocu, *n.m.,* parish priest

parrati, *2d pl. pres.ind of*
parrari, to speak

parratu, *past part. of* parrari,
to speak

parrari, *vb.,* to speak

partenza, *n. f.,* departure

parti, *n.f.,* part, side

partiri, *vb.,* to leave, depart

paru, *n.m.,* pair

passari, *vb.,* to pass, spend

passatu, *adj.,* passed

passaporto, *n.m,* passport

pasta, *n.f.,* pasta

pasta dentifricia, *n.f.,* toothpaste

patati ô furnu, *nounal
phrase,* roasted potatoes

patenti, *n.f.,* license

patri, *n.m,* father

paura, *n.f.,* fear

pedi, *n.m,* foot

peggiu, *adj.,adv.,* worse

pendenza, *n.f.,* slope

perciò, *conj.,* therefore

perdiri, *vb.,* to lose

permettiti *2d pl., pres ind.of*
permettiri, to permit

pî, *prep.* for the (pl.)

piaciri, *n.m,* pleasure; *vb.* to
like

piattu, *n.m,* plate, dish

picciottu, *n.m,* boy

picciridda, *n. f.,* little girl

picculu, *adj.,* small, short

pigghiamu *1st pl. pres.ind.of*
pigghiari, *vb.,* to get,

pigghiari, *vb.,* to get, take

pi(r),pri, *prep.,* for, through

pirchì, *conj.,* for, because,
so that (in order that)

pirsuna, *n. f.,* person

piru, *n.m,* pear tree, pira, *n. f.*
pear

pisci, *n.m,* fish

pisci spata, *n.m,* sword fish

pisci stoccu, *n.m,* stockfish

pitanza, *n. f.,*dish, delicacy

pitanzi, *n. f.,* foods

patruna, *n. f.,* patron, owner

pitturiscu, *adj.,* picturesque

pocu, *pron., adj.,* little, a bit

poi , *adv.* then

porcu , *n.m*, pig

porgi , *3d s. pres.ind.of*
   porgiri , to hand, give

postu , *n.m*, place, seats

poviru , *adj.*, poor

pranzari , *vb.*, to have lunch

pranzu , *n.m*, lunch

prefirisciu, *1st s.pres.ind.*
   prefiriri , to prefer

prenutari , *vb.*, to reserve

prenutu , *1st s.pres.ind.*
   prenutari , to reserve

prestu , *adv.*, soon

prezzu , *n.m*, price

priggiuni , *n. f.*, the prison

prima di , *prep.*, before (time)

prima chi , *conj.*, before

primu,-a , *adj.*, first

principali , *adj.*, principal

priparari , *vb.*, to prepare

prisintari , *vb.*, to present,
   introduce

professuri (profissuri), *n.m*,
   teacher

prontu , *adj.*, ready

propriu , *adv.* exactly, just as

proponi , *3d s. pres.ind.of*
   proponiri, to propose

prossimu , *pron.*, the next

prumettu , *1st s. pres.ind.of*
   prumettiri , to promise

pruvari , *vb.*, to try

pû(pir+ u), *prep.* for the

pueta , *n.m*, poet

pulitu , *adj.*, clean, neat

pumidamuri , *n.m*, tomato

pumu , *n.m*, apple tree, puma,
   n. f., apple

puntu , *n.m*, place, location

puru, *conj.*, too

pueta, *n.m.,* poet

purchì , *conj.*, provided that

puru, *conj.*, also

pusari , *vb.*, pause, stop

putemu , *1st pl., pres ind.*
   putiri , to be able to

putia , *n. f.*, shop

putiti *2d pl., pres ind.* putiri ,
   to be able to

qualchi , *adj.*, some,

qualcunu, *pron.*, anybody

qualchicosa , *pron,* anything

qualchidunu, *pron.*, anybody

quali , *pron.*, which

quasi , *adv.*, almost

qualsiasi , *adj.*, any

qualunqui , *pron.*, whatever

quannu , *conj.*, when

quannu , di, *prep.*, since

quantu , *pron.*, as much as,
   how much

quantu a, *prep.*, as to

quartu, *adj.*, fourth

quinto , *adj.*, fifth

R

raccumanna, *3d s. pres.ind.of*
  raccumannari to
  recommend

ragiuni, *n. f.*, reason

rammaricu, *n.m.*, sorrow

rammintari, *vb.* to remember,
  recall

ranni, *adj.*, big, large

rapprisintanti, *n.m.*, agent

re, *n.m.*, king

riccu, *adj.*, rich

ricetta, *n. f.*, recipe

riggina, *n. f.*, queen

riloggiu, *n.m.*, watch

rinomatu, *adj.*, renowned

ripusari, *vb.*, to rest

risicu, *n.m.*, risk

rispunniri, *vb.*, to answer,
  respond

ristoranti, *n.m.*, restaurant

ristoratu, *adj.*, restored

ritrattu, *n.m.*, picture, frame

riturnanu, *3d pl. pres.ind.of*
  riturnari, to return

romanu, *adj.*, Roman

rotunnu, *adj.*, round

russu, *adj.*, red

S

sacciu, *1st s. pres.ind.of*
  sapiri, to know

sai, *2nd s. pres.ind.of* **sapiri**,
  to know

sala da pranzu, *n. f.*, dining
  room

sala di biddizza, *n. f.*, beauty
  parlor

salottu, *n.m.*, living room

saluti, *n. f.*, health

santa, *n. f.*, saint

Santu, *n.m., adj.* Saint

sapi, *3d s. pres.ind.of* **sapiri**,
  to know

sapuri, *n.m.*, taste

sapuritu,-a, *adj.*, tasty

Saracenu, *n.m.*, Saracen

sardi, *n. f.*, (fresh) sardines

sarsa, *n. f.*, sauce

sarvaggiu, *adj.*, wild

sasizza, *n. f.*, sausage

scappanu, *3d pl. pres.ind.of*
  scappari, to escape, flee

scarpa, *n.f.*, shoe

scherzi, *2nd s.pres.ind.of*
  scherzari, to joke

sciacquari, *vb*, to rinse

sciaschicceddu, *n.m.* (shah
  skee CHEY doo), small flask

sciura, *n. f.*, flower

scola, *n. f.*, school

scrittu, *n.m.*, the writing

scritturi, *n.m.*, writer, author

scriviri, *vb*, to write

scunfiggitu, *past part.*
  scunfiggiri, to defeat

scutu, *n.m.*, dollar

scusatimi , excuse me

sebbeni , *conj.*, although

s *eculu* , *n.m.*, century

secunnariu , *pron.*, second
(dish)

secunnu , *adj.*, second; *prep.*,
according to

sedi , *n f.*, seat

seggia , *n. f.*, chair

seguiri , *vb.*, to follow

sempri , *adv.*, always

semu *1st pl. pres.ind.of* essiri ,
to be

senza , *prep.*, without

si , *pron.*, himself, herself,
themselves (m.,f.)

si (se), *conj.*, if, whether

sì , *adv.*, yes

siccomu , *conj.*, as (since)

Siciliani ,*n.m.*, Sicilians

signura , *n f.*, woman, lady

silenziusu , *adj.*, silent

simana , *n f.*, week

simenza , *n f.*, seed

sincerità , *n f.*, sincerity

sinistra , *pron.*, left side

sintiti , *2nd pl. pres.ind.of*
sentiri , to listen

sinu , *prep.*, up to

siti , *2nd pl. pres.ind.of* essiri ,
to be

so ,sò , *adj. pron.*, his, her,their

sofà , *n.m.*, sofa

sopratuttu , *adv.*, above all

soru , *n f.*, sister

specchiu , *n.m.*, mirror

speciali , *adj.*, special

specializza *3d s. pres. ind.of*
specializzari

Spagna , *n. f,* Spain

specii , *n.m.*, kinds

spiaggia , *n. f.*, beach

spissu , *adv.*, often

splennenti , *adj.*, brilliant

sposa , *n f.*, wife

spremuta , *n f.*, squeezed juice

sta , *adj.*, this

stamatina , *n f.*, this morning

stanza , *n f.*, room

stasira , *n f.*, tonight

stamatina , *adv.*, this morning

stampa *3d s. pres.ind.of*
stampari , to stamp

stanchi ,*adj.*, tired (pl)

stanza , *n f.*, room

stanza du bagnu , *n. f.*,
bathroom

stari , *vb.*, to stay, be, look

strana , *adj.*, strange

stancu, -a , *adj,* tired

str *ascicu* , *n.m.*, train (of a
dress)

stasira , *adv.*, this evening

statua , *n f.*, statue

stissa , *adj., pron.* same

st *oricu* , *adj,* historic

156

strata, *n. f.,* street
stratali, *adj.,* street
st*o*macu, *n.m.,* stomach
stanotti, *adv.,* last night
stu, *adj.m,* this
stu [chistu], *adj.,*this, this one
studia, *3d s. pres.ind.of*
   studiari, to study
su, *prep.,* on
su, *adj., m.,* that
sugnu, *1st s.. pres.ind.of*
   essiri, to be
sulu, *adv.,* only
sun(n)u, *3d pl. pres.ind.of*
   essiri ,to be
supra, *prep.,* above, on, over
sutta, *prep.,* below, under
T
tali, *pron.,* such, so, like
tal*i*a *3d s. pres.ind.& 2nd imp*
  of **taliari**, to look
tassa, *n. f.,* tax, toll
tassí, *n.m.,* taxi
tassista, *n.m.,* taxi driver
tantu...comu, *adv.,* as...as
tantu menu, *conj.,* much less
tantu ...quantu, *adv.,* as...as
ta*v*ula, *n. f.,* table
teatru, *n.m.,* theater
tel*e*fonu, *n.m.,* telephone
telegramma, *n.m.,* telegram
tempu, *n.m.,* time
terra, *n. f.,* earth

terzu, *adj.,* third
testa, *n. f.,* head
ti, *pron.,* yourself, to you
t*i*a,*subj. pron.,* you
t*i*picu, *adj.,*typical
tipu, *n.m.,* type, kind
ten*i*ri, *vb.,* to keep, to hold
to,tò, *adj., pron.,* your, yours
tornanu, *3d pl. pres.ind.of*
   tornari, to turn, return
t*o*ssicu, *n.m.,* toxic
tra, *prep.,*within
tra*f*icu, *n.m.,* trade
tranni, *prep.,* except
tra*s*inu, *3d pl. pres.ind.of*
   tra*s*iri, to enter
tratta, *3d s. pres.ind.of*
   trattari, to deal with
trattturi*a*, *n.m.,* small
  restaurant
travagghia, *3d s. pres.ind.of*
   travagghia ri, to work
trentina, *n. f,* about thirty
troppu, *adj.,* too much, too
truvari, *vb.,* to find
tu, *pron., 2nd s.,* you
tubettu, *n.m.,* tube
turista, *n.m.,* tourist
turnari, *vb.,* to return
tuttavia, *conj.,* however
tuttu, *adj., pron.* all
tutti, *pron.,* everyone
tutti i dui, *pron.,* both

U

u, [**lu**], *def.art.,m., sing.*, **i**, [**li**] *p*l, the, it
ucchiata , *n. f.*, glance
ufficiali , *n.m.*, officer
un,-a , *indef. art., pron.*one
università , *n. f.*, university
unn [**non**], *adv.*, no, not
unni [**unna**], *adv.*, *conj.*,where
unni , **di**, *conj.*, whence
unu, *ind.art.*, **one** (**l'unu e l'autru** , *pron.*,both)
ura, *n. f*, hour
usari , *vb.*, to use

V

valliggetta , *n. f*, valise
valigia (**-i**) , *n. f*, valise(s)
valiri , *vb.*, to be worth
varva , *n. f.*, beard
vasca du bagnu , *n. f*, bathtub
vayu , *1st.s. pres.ind.of* **iri**, to go
vecchiu , *adj.*, old
veni , *3d s. pres.ind.of* **veniri**, to come
veniri , *vb.*, to come
versu , *prep.*, toward
veru , *adj.*, true
vestirsi , *vb.*, to dress oneself
vi , *pron.*, to you, for you, yourselves
via , *n. f.*, road, way

viaggiari , *vb.*, to travel
viaggiu , *n.m.*, trip
vicinu , *adv.*, nearby
vicinu a , *prep.*, near
vidiri, *vb.*, to see
vidu , *3d s. pres. ind.of* **vidiri**, to see
vin icula , *adj.*,wine
viniti , *2d pl., pres.ind..of* **veniri** , to come
vintina , *n. f.*, about twenty
vinu , *n.m.*,wine
virità , *n. f.*, truth
virtù , *n. f*, virtue
visitari , *vb.*, to visit
visitatu , *past part. of* **visitari** , to visit
vista , *n. f*, view
vistina , *n. f.*, dress
vistu , *n.m.*, visa
vistu , *past part.*, **vidiri**, to see
vistuariu , *n.m.*, clothing
volu , *n.m.*, flight
vostru ,*adj.*, your
vota , *n. f.*, turn, time
vuautri [**vui, voss ia**], *pron.*,you
vucca , *n. f.*, mouth
vulcanu , *n.m.*,volcano
vulemu *3d pl., pres.ind..of* **vuliri** , to want

vulissi , *imp.subj. of* **vuliri**
(you, he,she) would want
vuliti , *2d pl., pres.ind..of*
vuliri , to want
vuliri beni , to love

vulunteri , *adv.,* willingly
vutti , *n. f,* barrel

Z

zaccu , *pron.*, what, that which
ziu , *n.m.,* uncle

ITALIAN-ENGLISH/ ENGLISH-ITALIAN DICTIONARY

New Edition-with larger Print

This dictionary is a compilation of over 35,000 entries for students and travelers. It also includes a phonetic guide to pronunciation in both languages, a handy glossary of menu terms, bilingual instruction on how-to-use the dictionary, a bilingual list of irregular verbs, and a bilingual list of abbreviations.

Italian Interest from Hippocrene...

ITALIAN-ENGLISH/ENGLISH-ITALIAN PRACTICAL DICTIONARY, Large Print Edition
488 pages • 5 1/2 x 8 1/4 • 35,000 entries • 0-7818-0354-3 • W • $9.95pb • (201)

ITALIAN HANDY DICTIONARY
120 pages • 5 x 7 3/4 • 0-7818-0011-0 • USA • $8.95pb • (196)

MASTERING ITALIAN
360 pages • 5 1/2 x 8 1/2 • 0-87052-057-1 • USA • $11.95pb • (517)
2 Cassettes: 0-87052-066-0 • USA • $12.95 • (521)

MASTERING ADVANCED ITALIAN
278 pages • 5 1/2 x 8 1/2 • 0-7818-0333-0 • W • $14.95pb • (160)
2 Cassettes: 0-7818-0334-9 • W • $12.95 • (161)

TREASURY OF ITALIAN LOVE
128 pages • 5 x 7 • 0-7818-0352-7 • W • $11.95hc • (587)

TREASURY OF ITALIAN LOVE AUDIO CASSETTES
2 cassettes: 0-7818-0366-7 • W • $12.95 • (581)

DICTIONARY OF 1000 ITALIAN PROVERBS
131 pages • 5 1/2 x 8 1/2 • 0-7818-0458-2 • W • $11.95pb • (370)

Sicilian
SICILIAN-ENGLISH/ ENGLISH-SICILIAN CONCISE DICTIONARY
210 pages • 4 x 6 • 4,000 entries • 0-7818-0457-4 • W • $11.95pb • (422)

Hippocrene's Beginner's Series...

Do you know what it takes to make a phone call in Russia? Or how to get through customs in Japan? This new language instruction series shows how to handle oneself in typical situations by introducing the business person or traveler not only to the vocabulary, grammar, and phrases of a new language, but also the history, customs, and daily practices of a foreign country.

The Beginner's Series consists of basic language instruction, which also includes vocabulary, grammar, and common phrases and review questions, along with cultural insights, interesting historical background, the country's basic facts and hints about everyday living, driving, shopping, eating out, and more.

Arabic For Beginners
188 pages • 5 ¼ x 8 ¼ • 0-7818-01141 • $9.95pb • (18)

Beginner's Chinese
150 pages • 5 ½ x 8 • 0-7818-0566-x • $14.95pb • (690)

Beginner's Bulgarian
207 pages • 5 ½ x 8 ½ • 0-7818-0300-4 • $9.95pb • (76)

Beginner's Czech
200 pages • 5 ½ x 8 ½ • 0-7818-0231-8 • $9.95pb • (74)

Beginner's Esperanto
400 pages • 5 ½ x 8 ½ • 0-7818-0230-x • $14.95pb • (51)

Beginner's Hungarian
200 pages • 5 ½ x 7 • 0-7818-0209-1 • $7.95pb • (68)

Beginner's Japanese
200 pages • 5 ½ x 8 ½ • 0-7818-0234-2 • $11.95pb • (53)

Beginner's Maiori
121 pages • 5 ½ x 8 ½ • 0-7818-0605-4 • $8.95pb • (703)

Beginner's Persian
150 pages • 5 ½ x 8 • 0-7818-0567-8 • $14.95pb • (696)

Beginner's Polish
200 pages • 5 ½ x 8 ½ • 0-7818-0299-7 • $9.95pb • (82)

Beginner's Romanian
200 pages • 5 ½ x 81/2 • 0-7818-0208-3 • $7.95pb • (79)

Beginner's Russian
200 pages • 5 ½ x 8 ½ • 0-7818-0232-6 • $9.95pb • (61)

Beginner's Swahili
200 pages • 5 ½ x 8 ½ • 0-7818-0335-7 • $9.95pb • (52)

Beginner's Ukrainian
130 pages • 5 ½ x 8 ½ • 0-7818-0443-4 • # $11.95pb • (88)

Beginner's Vietnamese
517 pages • 7 x 10 • 30 lessons • 0-7818-0411-6 • $19.95pb • (253)

Beginner's Welsh
210 pages • 5 ½ x 8 ½ • 0-7818-0589-9 • $9.95pb • (712)

MORE about our Mastering Series...

These imaginative courses, designed for both individual and classroom use, assume no previous knowledge of the language. The unique combination of practical exercises and step-by-step grammar emphasizes a functional approach to new scripts and their vocabularies. Everyday situations and local customs are explored variously through dialogues, newspaper extracts, drawings and photos. Cassettes are available for each language.

MASTERING ARABIC
320 pp • 5 ¼ x 8 ¼ • 0-87052-922-8 • USA • $14.95pb • (501)
2 cassettes: 0-87052-984-8 • (507)

MASTERING FINNISH
278 pp • 5 ½ x 8 ½ • 0-7818-0233-4 • W • $14.95pb • (184)
2 Cassettes: 0-7818-0265-2 • W • $12.95 • (231)

MASTERING FRENCH
288 pp • 5 ½ x 8 ½ • 0-87052-055-5 USA • $14.95pb • (511)
2 Cassettes: • 0-87052-060-1 USA • $12.95 • (512)

MASTERING ADVANCED FRENCH
348 pp • 5 ½ x 8 ½ • 0-7818-0312-8 • W • $14.95pb • (41)
2 Cassettes: • 0-7818-0313-8 • W • $12.95 • (54)

MASTERING GERMAN
340 pp • 5 ½ x 8 ½ • 0-87052-056-3 USA • $11.95pb • (514)
2 Cassettes: • 0-87052-061-X USA • $12.95 • (515)

MASTERING ITALIAN
360 pp • 5 ½ x 8 ½ • 0-87052-057-1 • USA • $11.95pb • (517)
2 Cassettes: 0-87052-066-0 • USA • $12.95 • (521)

MASTERING ADVANCED ITALIAN
278 pp • 5 ½ x 8 ½ • 0-7818-0333-0 • W • $14.95pb • (160)
2 Cassettes: 0-7818-0334-9 • W • $12.95 • (161)

MASTERING JAPANESE
368 pp • 5 ½ x 8 ½ • 0-87052-923-4 • USA • $14.95pb • (523)
2 Cassettes: • 0-87052-983-8 USA • $12.95 • (524)

MASTERING NORWEGIAN
183 pp • 5 ½ x 8 ½ • 0-7818-0320-9 • W • $14.95pb • (472)

MASTERING POLISH
288 pp • 5 ½ x 8 ½ • 0-7818-0015-3 • W • $14.95pb • (381)
2 Cassettes: • 0-7818-0016-1 • W • $12.95 • (389)

MASTERING RUSSIAN
278 pp • 5 ½ x 8 ½ • 0-7818-0270-9 • W • $14.95pb • (11)
2 Cassettes: • 0-7818-0271-7 • W • $12.95 • (13)

MASTERING SPANISH
338 pp • 5 ½ x 8 ½ • 0-87052-059-8 USA • $11.95 • (527)
2 Cassettes: • 0-87052-067-9 USA • $12.95 • (528)

MASTERING ADVANCED SPANISH
326 pp • 5 ½ x 8 ½ • 0-7818-0081-1 • W • $14.95pb • (413)
2 Cassettes: • 0-7818-0089-7 • W • $12.95 • (426)